How Lean is Lean

The Wealth in Nations

How Lean is Lean?

I0403910

Dr. Madhavi C Vasanta

How Lean is Lean

Acknowledgements

I thank all my consultants and boards to give me the knowledge on their existing business preferences and social relatedness of issues for firms and economy.

Disclaimer

The book is a product of business knowledge, views and experience. All contents are aimed at discussion and feedback without any responsibility for claims or authority of the views.

Not to sound passé, the credit is ours and the mistakes are mine. Thank you for making it a part of your read.

Intro: The Opening Dialogue

'…it has been over six months and my company identified honing points like expenses, manpower, costs, etc. to tone down… now we have 20% growth in profitability and revenues…,' said Rewam, VP of GMI.

'…but what does it mean? Does that really translate into more from less? If your revenues have grown by 20% then how can profits be with same growth when expenses are down too… if not by more than 20%, then it is not lean… if yes, then profits should be growing by more than so ever…,' said Klen, a SVP from a competitor firm Tell.

The above is a common debate where companies cannot claim to be experts

How Lean is Lean

as the union of numbers is hardly a reality. It happens only in formulae. Real financials show a figurative state of the firm that is liable and vulnerable to lot of loopholes.

The numbers in sales, both volumes and revenues, are deviant to end from start. They may come from a varying source as very many times they stem from the new customer base built up or one-off client by luck. This is the reason why the business volatility too comes in.

The expenses and manpower seem to be always on the chopping arenas. But how much is it true? Companies claim to be lean by lean, and leaner by leanest but that is not so easy. The lean is defined on the buffer of variances from actuals or 'ideal' numbers. Today our business has flourished to overcome the

How Lean is Lean

lean barriers as we employ and deploy only the best men and technologies.

At the same time, today the business is growing in multi-directional path where it is difficult to really fathom the lean actual vs. must-be's.

The men are retained some times, fired sometimes, hired most of the times, retrained, cross-employed, and business needs are re-assessed each time. The staff requirements are first of all not always accurately determined. There needs to be a proper measurement of need. Here's where numbers make sense and meaning. The business needs are most comfortably stated and in English by escaping the number of the related need. That far it is easy to manage but the problem comes when people are blamed or hyped on

How Lean is Lean

the same stated goals. We need to add or boost the employee strength – is the management goal. It is purely subjective and no manager can win on the account whether she hire 1 or 100. In today's business the other extreme of lean is construed to mean subjectivity as objectivity in that the strength is actually due on the training and skills. So fire 2 but train few employees to add a skill or two. This is erroneous interpretation of lean. Definitions are many but I am not going into those. Practical errors are more minor than theoretical. Correcting them is easy and effective for the business rather than brushing up theories. A change in the word can alter the definition hugely. Hence it sounds better to work with the business than book. Past is more important in lean always. Companies cannot thrive on forecasts. They have to elucidate the past success and failures to make the

How Lean is Lean

lean improvements. The areas are not just staff and expenses as is most often misconstrued. The lean is for the decision-making, momentum of action-plans, speed of strategy execution, commitment to growth (uni-multi directional). Where not to be lean is also important in making full use of lean business. The firms cannot run with the resources endlessly. They have to relax the rules with customers. Companies cannot be lean with customers saying that only 3 calls per customer per day on their issues or only $1 per customer. The first hurdle is that once you make such a decision your company is not counting on customers anymore. You have to decide where not to get lean. The second hurdle is that a firm cannot but overrun on costs somewhere or the other due to the stringent unnecessary changes in work styles created on such false expectations. Leakages are bound

How Lean is Lean

to happen in lean on such false premises. Intermediate changes can cause unwarranted tasks and false projects to earn leakages in lean. It's a fact that no company runs on cost-effective projects only. There are many other projects that keep a company stick to its guns. The non-customer projects are also many and they are not really loss-makers as they earn resources, revenues and projects for future indirectly. The amount of lean involved in projects depends on the start and transition. It may begin lean and then seniors cannot force you to tailor it further, the crash line to degradation also starts there. Hence it needs to be studied well to understand how much is lean, where is lean required and why not. Making lean projects lean can get them no lean. They won't be able to achieve targets and would become only burden on the company. They would

How Lean is Lean

neither be able to survive nor add value to the work. The Managers and Teams would only debate over essentials rather than performance in such lean assignments. They would not be able to verify whether the lean is really lean or only a way to praise up in the appraisals or a forced blind approach. It can be top-down or bottom-up and not just one as we feel. We can start lean at any time and not only at the start or end of a value-chain. So force no pretexts on lean business as the business is lean as long as the constituents are. The constituents of lean are the lean cycle, boosters, toners and next lean. It is important to know what to do after lean as firms mostly feel happy at cutting down the costs but don't know how to utilize the saved lines. Toners enable business fitness by not just pruning costs, but adding weight where needed, like more cost on quality, inspection

How Lean is Lean

related to strategy or technology to save time. Boosters should not be taken as sudden or magic steps to improve sales or business performance. Lean cycle is the process of lean and it indicates the demarcation between the extra line and lean line. The extra line is the line of non-lean as not any more useful to the business when the lean is exceeded. The lean line is the measure of the range which is considered to be lean. There cannot be point lean as business is an entity and it cannot function at a single point in time but over a period of time. The process of lean and next lean determines the milestones of lean. The measures of lean are not just in the numbers coming down but the numbers going up too. The contradictions in Lean are not one but many. How can companies grow when there is low resource level? Why cannot lean companies win in the business in true

How Lean is Lean

sense? Why is lean not so lean? There is a difference between flourishing bet and bet and flailing bet. In fact there are more than what we think for lean levels. The first one is the extra-heavy business, medium business, normal business, small business and agile business.

It simply cannot be lean if not done on time. Management must assess when to get lean and when not. Business diagnostics are able to bring the sick ones out and ignoring can throw the good ones into red. Companies waste time and resources on redundant effort on reducing costs or expenses always. But that is not the real drama as it only shows ways of circumventing the failure. The inefficiency lays somewhere else and not in expenses. It is in the work ethics or the employee incontinence. Some bosses leave it to their subordinates to achieve targets by hook

How Lean is Lean

or crook. This is not the right approach of delegation. The work had to follow certain ethics earlier and now also it must. Deviations result in wrong problem-identification and erroneous solutions proposal. Firms do not work on the required dimensions but pile up things of interest. Costs are not always the concerns in today's context at least. Companies have the frontal problem of selling. Earlier we used to come from the back working on the internal expense reduction etc. The back-on-front approach is no more valid. Today we need a frontal-attack leading to internal adjustments. The simple difference is that earlier companies could sell what they made; today they make what they can sell. This is the only thing that works with companies as otherwise the products would be adding to the costs if not needed in the stores. This is not just to say that people would

How Lean is Lean

always need what they ask for. Sometimes markets reveal products that are in demand but not really needed. The daily use newspapers are in demand but new brands are not needed. Still publishers launch new newspapers. This is mostly due to the over-abundance of brands and varieties. Unless an explosively new brand comes up with an extremely different feature nobody needs any of the products existing in the markets. The varieties are many but the buyers are few. The new products coming in the market also are not able to last longer. The functionality is short-lived as people are bored of the monotony in products. A product seems to be innovative because of the name, ad, or aesthetics. After a use it turns out to be the same as many others. This is true of the cell phones. Every phone is labelled as different but they are all the same. Markets don't sell what they don't

How Lean is Lean

understand. Customers don't understand what markets don't sell. Hence for companies to be winning at all times, they should sell and understand to make the customers buy and understand what the products are and how they fit their needs. Age-old saying is to treat customer as the king but not the king as customer. Now it is needed that you treat everyone as your customer. Then you do the best and sell what you otherwise cannot. Banks say that how they get new wealthy customers is important for them, along with more interest income on lending. Firms say that how many buyers they get for their products or consumers using their products is important. Services firms say that the number of reprise meetings they get from each customer is important to their business. Creating opportunities is more important for each customer rather than waiting.

How Lean is Lean

Customers create their opportunities by identifying the weak points for sellers. They get promotional offers or discounts based on the company's approach. Each company differs in the sales pattern owing to its promotional tactics. Some companies stop at the conversion of a sale. Others stop at understanding the customers. Few stop at the meeting itself. It depends on what level of growth the company is at any given point in time. a mature firm goes for after-sale experience, growing firms go for sales per se, intermediate firms go for making a sale, nascent firms go for the customer attention. Like this the company may lose customers at any stage. But customer does not lose a company that she wants for her hi-life. Her family depends on a company and the use continues until a better option is available in the market for good. The products many try for once or twice are

How Lean is Lean

only for comparison or change. The reliable or good products never lose their loyalty in the houses.

As one company competes with another there is also a hidden competition between customers. It is not clear but very subtle if companies can make out the patterns of buyers. Buyers compete among themselves like customers vying for others' attention. It is not just social status but the personal attitudes that get shaped by the use of products. They show to the other customers how a product has shaped their kids' life or they observe in others how their product has affected the development of their spouses' career. This is all on a single product. A product is hence more powerful than a company or firm. A brand is more powerful than a product. It creates an ever-lasting impact on the

How Lean is Lean

buyer's use of the products if they do not declare satisfactory. It is not that great a result if it is the best product. It has to be best to be in the market. A customer or company are only as important as their needs or products.

Contents

1. Numbers
2. The X-tremes of Lean
3. Simple to Practise, Tough to Learn
4. Where not to be Lean
5. Leakages in Lean
6. Lean Improvements
7. Why Lean is only not Lean
8. The Lean Line
9. The Lean Constituents - lean cycle, boosters, toners, next lean
10. Projects and non-Customer Projects
11. Milestones in Lean
12. Timing the Lean
13. Lean times vs. Now or Then
14. Lean impact on Sales
15. Everyone's a Customer
16. Customers compete
17. Who is a Customer?
18. Lean Employees

How Lean is Lean

1 – Numbers

Companies should not be bothered much about the numbers as they seem to be. Nobody can do much about a missed sale and this should be stamped on the mind. It only creates a wrong impression on salesmen that some can convince but others cannot. It's a chance on how the sales communications can make an impact on the buyer. You as a buyer won't buy even if the seller uses Latin English or Roman English or dresses up like Lord Curzon or looks into your eyes like a freedom fighter. You would buy if you are ok with the features of a product and if you feel like buying at that time. it

How Lean is Lean

comes from your background and not your pitcher's. If you had a fight with your spouse you won't buy for her or buy to please her. Why would you buy if the salesman had a good day with his wife or a bad day with his boss? It's his life and doesn't affect your purchase decision. Hence these wrong allusions should be removed as nobody cares about others but yourself. The same is true of targets. Salesmen always try their best whether they fight at home or not. Some are dumb by birth and some are smart by birth. Or you can say that training can make them so. Over-training can make them dumb as it has been seen in the past that those who spend more time on desk than field are less competitive and slow with work. They work for the sake of working by adhering to what is given and skipping what is not. An overall employee is one who fights for the company and

How Lean is Lean

achieves the target. Even if she does not achieve the target she is still a victor because she knows the in and out of the business. Such a male employee is also worthy because he is confident of meeting dozens of different propellers of business without much preparation.

No company has won on the back of numbers only. Market leaders do not become so by working on the hard numbers or starting their day with sales and ending with numbers. Business is much more than sales or money. Numerics are for measuring the business but not for judging the measures. Employees are the measure and their achievements are the numbers. They should be made to strive for numbers only as long as they can add value to the business. Selling a thousand more ships does not add to

How Lean is Lean

my business value as selling a single idea to a single or many customers. What is our gain? The more customers buy into a company's idea, the more they bring in attention. In today's world, it's all the game of eyeballs. The more attention you get, the more good resources come to you. And then you know what is good for your business. If you cannot understand your employees then you cannot understand your customers. Also, numbers are only ways to trap logic. They are not meant for guiding the entire team to run behind them. Chasing numbers is easier than chasing men but users of business are men and not numbers. This is thus a completely reversal of business for the wrong means. Lean does not mean reducing numbers. That is why lean is not always lean also. It may mean adding numbers. At times when business is not selling adequate

How Lean is Lean

products, it has to add to the expense of branding exercise to prevail its name in the market. Or else the top-of-the-mind recall is gone from the customer's heads. We do not get the business running all the time. If the cost has to be reduced as per the lean definition then the lean has to apply to the cost of stacking up resources when the firm is not selling products. Otherwise lean is like kill. Too lean would kill the business. Cut on the expenses to the extent that the business cannot survive. The expenses that your firm incurs may actually be less than needed. The numbers there fore can misguide you if not interpreted in the right direction. Business experts have to understand the necessary and unnecessary Math in business.

How Lean is Lean

The line of profit and sales is valid only as much as the credibility and product are built on the customers. They don't bother to buy because you have cut down on all costs. It is hardly a business sale proposition hence. The firms sometimes blindly work on numbers, assign them to the sales team and leave it to flourish as if it is the norm of business existence. Because others are doing that wont help you in any way. Your business has to follow your model and not other's. It is just a chance if the model seems to work and you crack sales for some time.

The business has to become independent in the long or short term. Numbers don't make it independent. To some extent they are needed because otherwise employees are like goats gazing the grasses. They need to know

How Lean is Lean

where to go and how much to get. They have to fight for the rates and volumes. If he can sell two today he has to try for four next day. IF you don't tell the employees to sell, they wont try to sell. So that message has to go but not as a strict train of numbered bogies. The numbers can help them only as much as they can study them. They cannot make them excel if they don't know the relevance.

The numbers are relevant only as far as the customers. Most companies work on numbers alone. They punish employees for not meeting the numbers or for not understanding the numbers. They ignore the customers or preserve them for the end. Solutions don't come if we attend to customers in the end. Like a magic formula, they are not the cops who come at the end of the gauntlet.

How Lean is Lean

They have to be now, then and every time with the company. Lean numbers only mean clear and direct costs without including many middlemen and without complicating the interpretations. Each salesman gets a target to sell 5 cars per day. Whether they meet or not, it's their personal growth that gets affected. Their job is to let the company survive with the customers. A non-buyer is not a non-customer. She is also your customer and needs to be taken care of well. Anybody who uses your company as a patron or habitué through direct purchase or use or indirect following or comparison is a customer. Let the company not get lost in numbers but use them as meek figures in a heavy work. A lot of work and few numbers make sense. A lot of numbers and no work does not.

How Lean is Lean

There are lot of numbers related to finances, market volumes, customer sales, supply-chain costs, travel dynamics, returns, exchanges, refunds and call-backs. These numbers happen at different stages of a business cycle. Hence they cannot be generalized or peeked at while the employees are working. A business is a multi-vitiated growth process. It cannot be timed as such. No two employees perform at equal levels, so they must be evaluated at different sticks. A number may be good for one but not the other worker. A number may make sense to some employees while not to others. Numbers drag the business in one direction while the employee tends to drag it in a different one. It's acceptable a while if the drags can create a business opportunity otherwise the business becomes laggard.

How Lean is Lean

If managers investigate they get to know that a single deal is a result of multiple teams and not one person. Hence one person cannot be levied with humongous calculations. The numbers apply to teams but a single person cannot construe in the same way as a company. They create tension on others leading to breakdowns, failing relations, sour decisions etc. A company that becomes lean not by counting but by working is the real one that gives strength to it in the long-term. Numbers can or cannot fit the realities as we know that markets are volatile cups that can vaporize in no time. If a company sits in it as a number it will be gone in no time. If a firm sits in it as a business it will be hard to vaporise as then an entity would have people, numbers, machines and others. We started with Men, Material and Money. Today we have Machines, Material and Money. Still

How Lean is Lean

men are not gone. They work with machines. But their presence is related less than earlier times. Does it mean that we do away with them? No. Similarly not going by numbers does not mean that we are putting them off fully. In future we would be more reliant on Machines, Material and Meaning. The last one would cover numbers, men, and other Ms. The business meaning is defeated if we cannot use numbers sensibly. The companies keep telling that they want to make decisions mainly on numbers or analysts would juggle with numbers in their commentaries. But the numbers are not the only judges or mentors. Because of the simple reason that they are not understood by all... a lot of us understand and all of us know numbers. But the relevance to business is debatable. Not all numbers are presented and quoted in the right way by all employees. Some stick to them,

How Lean is Lean

some use them while others ignore them. Cutting down the cost by 50% and not doing any efficiency is like a meatless plate for a carnivore.

An herbivore appreciates it but you know what I mean. It is like no meat for lion. Then a lion is not a lion. If a firm does not produce enough with 100% capacity but wastes time on reducing the headcount, it loses its men who could create customers, new products and grow business. It is like protein-free meat diet. A carnivore does not gain anything by eating that just as business cannot. The growth happened by numbers in the past and will continue to remain so but in the books. That is for measurement and not daily routines. The numbers are for comparisons of deficits or excesses but when employees sit on counting every day,

How Lean is Lean

numbers can create stress to eat away their planning and next day's tasks. If they are more, they may be complacent. If they are low, they may be discouraged.

The growth of branches may be counted but leaning is not basing on numbers. Leaning means basing on hard facts and working with numbers. It means not manipulation but factual to estimate not ignoring estimates to actuals. Both ways have to be worked upon to derive the methods of business success.

Even the shareholders and investors and just not the customers are relevant along with employees. For a business to be splendid, the investors should get returns which they will get without fail if every complaint is addressed to success. Every part of the business had to be successful earlier to make the firm

How Lean is Lean

a sick-free unit. The business should function in full along with every participant and component in active growth.

The employees and resources if utilized to full cannot but render growth to business. If every particle of the business is happy then it cannot fail. The numbers also will turn into favour then. They do come in but after the business is done. They come once at the beginning and the end but the gap has to be on to make the business growing as growth doesn't happen in a day or year. You may argue that numbers cannot still keep the growth on as growth omits time. It comes and goes. It is discrete and not continuous. Exactly, more so, why numbers cannot make companies lean by showing low. This is not size zero or minus 1 to show the world of the firm size. It is never

How Lean is Lean

going to be thought so whether in real world or business world.

What your business does counts. What your desk, others, vendors, suppliers, buyers, sellers, distributors, competitors, employees, investors do counts. It simply cannot throw the blame onto numbers that all employees are known by numbers and nothing personal. Business is highly personal. The sales teams would not be functioning but for the rapports they develop. The client partners cannot boast of numbers of revenues if they stop talking to the customers in spite of making fantastic products. It's all in the game. The crystal ball wields power and it goes to men but not numbers. They cannot argue or fight or support the business decisions. The numbers are indicators and have to be there as the majestic rulers rather than

How Lean is Lean

managers. Managers negotiate numbers but not vice versa. How many managers can argue without the numbers? Many. Yes that is true. Many can work without them too. The numbers are meant to guide and not dictate. Because, that applies only if, there are serious lacunae between capabilities and expectations. You have to force numbers down the throats of the people as there's no other escape. Given that the world is progressing in a methodical and intellectual manner we need to not argue or rationalise the existence of workers by numbers.

They are able to understand the work ethics and client needs. The things have improved a lot from earlier. Today people irrespective of English or non can handle tasks with great efficiency and success. Numbers cannot rule

How Lean is Lean

unless completely entrusted to machines. This is not going to be possible in at least the next century. People have not given the freedom of thought and decision to machines. So they have to act as assistants and not as masters. Machines cannot be our bosses so numbers cannot make us lean. The business cannot run by counting on the number of machines, hours, expenses or products. It has created a whole balance between needs, clients, gaps, time and changes. It sounds not as simple though. The managers need to assist the business by making it flexible to market changes rather than adherent on few statistics. We cannot deduce the company success or excellence by saying that they simply sell the most. It is the last of all observations. First they have to go on proving as most well-versed in the business, then in the customers, then in

How Lean is Lean

the competition, then in the products, then in the technology, then in the sales, then in the quality, then in the marketing and branding. There are lot of things that fit in the line and we have to look at all those things. It also does not mean that the firms should take them in the same sequence. They are all on the top or equal for companies but the market will look at them late and not when we showcase them. Hence they should reflect all equally in our survival again why numbers cannot really guide them all unless ratified at the end. I don't say that you should ignore the numbers in the start and take them in the end.

Consider them in the beginning and plug them in the end spots.

Then compare in the end to identify the gaps and strengths. But do not project

How Lean is Lean

them as the tools, as they are measures of your business.

Leaning down the business by numbers is reducing the fat numbers too small for related heads. Volumes can be reduced if the overheads are more.

2 – The X-Tremes of Lean

Lean can be construed on intrinsic and extrinsic by taking the either ends of the spectrum. Companies usually try to balance the figures but lean can swing in any direction. If a company finds crunch its tendency is to make the lean on the lower end.

Everything can reach to ebb including manpower, costs, capacities etc. A firm that operates at lowest capacities to save on the related costs will ultimately save money in profits also. Machines will be conserved and resources will be preserved without using them for the business value. Value-addition will never come in the initial runs but after epicentre break-through.

How Lean is Lean

The company would make gains after all the losses happen and pruned to reach the optimum levels. The companies look for ways to cut down costs by adding methods, softwares and tools. The extra cost incurred on them is taken as another investment or return-prone spend. The revenue expenditures and capital expenditures are all that need to be checked before randomly working on lean reduction to avoid the tilting of the firm randomly on the low side. It is not easy to make up for the losses brought down to lean groups. Manpower cannot add on as quickly as it can be put off. Machines cannot regain capacities unless utilized consistently. Technologies cannot be made to function if not used regularly. There are many things, they cannot rediscover the efficiencies as quickly as earlier. They cannot fill in the gaps in given short times. The firms seem to function as

How Lean is Lean

normal but their internal processes are hampered beyond recognition. The employees cannot add to the day's routines if not made to understand them for long. A day cannot implement lean if it is on ebb. Lean functions on the optimization and not on gaining the extremes as thought by many managers. They feel that the lower the spending side, the leaner the firm is but that is not so. The lower the spending side, the lower the scope for business growth. Whatever spent is for customers and then it is value-addition. If whatever spent is for inefficient or lack of knowledge or expertise then it is on lean requirement side. The lean could build up on higher end if not carefully implemented. The expenses can boom to the higher side if not monitored well. When firms control costs they ignore the time. Future may present a position either to close or spend more. Then

How Lean is Lean

companies would choose the latter without saying. Companies mostly look at costs only whenever a new management tactic comes into play. This is wrong and peevish. If costs matter, other things also do. Lean was made to cut down the bottlenecks and not costs. Cost is a small part of lean. Lean was invented to make the business agile by losing its weight. Again cost orientation is due to leaning on numbers.

Any number that needs reduction means cost, any number that needs hype means revenue. This is very essential but not a realistic business approach. Extreme modern times take us back to traditional days. We are now at a near stage. We have to go back to those days when we saw business as a profession and not as a machine

How Lean is Lean

churning money. Today we are losing that focus and using lean on the business to make it diminish its importance. The business is pruned to such an extent that lean is minus costs, plus sales. Hence business definition is lean to money. No firm can run or add value this way. No firm can survive in any time using lean in this way. But how true is it not? Talk to any manager and she takes pride in showing the cost reductions and revenue additions. Frankly, this is not single man's job but team's. Otherwise, keep that person and fire others. That is what companies would do as no founder is blind to pay others for free. We know that such lean measures are not really lean as they don't add business value to the company. Just as we create value for customers, employees should create calculable value for the company also. A value that does not come from the

How Lean is Lean

employee is not leading to lean in the company. She has to contribute to the internal process refinement and customer approaches. She has to work on the costs and revenues but they are again the fallouts and not the processes per se. Sales and pre-sales are again not focus areas in lean, they are one of. It is not the job of every employee to increase sales. They come when clients want. Buyers are not rampant as they also spend 80% of their resources in purchase-reiki. They don't buy all of a sudden but understand the patterns, prices, trends, feedback of sellers.

They may buy, borrow or make for their use depending on the permanency or constancy of need. It's the same thing that firms also do when they hire on contractual or full-time or part-time basis. We also don't want to make

How Lean is Lean

markets crowded and flooded with resources or products. The products are the benchmarks against which all growth is measured and leaned.

When firms look at quality they measure lean as direct result in terms of defectives. This approach is reliable because it does not involve numbers like cost or sales but the product that is unbiased. It is balanced as this is where lean started long back.

Companies had to measure the acceptable and un- levels of defects. The products could not be passed on to the market if rejected by the internal inspectors and consumers. If a firm cannot claim its quality how can a customer vouch for it with another? Even before, how can employees showcase their quality if it is not passing internal tests? Deviating from this level

How Lean is Lean

takes lean to either extremes. The managers may say that it involves heavy cost to replace the given quality and it may be made to 'it's ok' or 'chalta hai' level with the slight offer or promotional package as it is not critical to hygiene or health.

The next move would be to project this internally in the firm and those involved in the value chain will strive to make it look so. It weakens the entire process and product branding. A lot of deviants will come saying, we should work on costs, or sales, or ads, or offers. The real focus of customer and quality would be lost. Men will be blamed as they have to be to be fired.

Resources will lose allocations as they will be misused or abused. Customer loyalty schemes will come and they will be made to use the products subsidised

How Lean is Lean

by heavy rewards. It will hurt innovation and market standards without a doubt. The firms cannot make standards but cannot increase them too if they don't let lean function on non-extremes. The employees would be seen getting certifications on the go and a lot of audits will go with the label lean or lean sigma but they cannot be really made to work with the appraisals claiming the real projects. Most projects are sowing seeds for the new concepts in firms but they go to the either ends before showing the real use of them. They are either shown as working in two or three projects with powerful numbers of high defects going to low; or as improvements in quality from grade b to A. But this is hardly the case as the interpretation is not with the subject. Firstly a project or two cannot be segregated for such initiatives. Lean is through the organization and not on one

How Lean is Lean

or two departments. It should run through the process and not on numbers. It has to be made a part of the business as-is and not to-be. It is not new too. We knew it without any label and now we learn it because there are so many other things to do in a company. Each had to be noted and checked to ensure that nothing is missed.

The companies need to nurture the spirit of lean without sticking to the ends of the horizon.

The horizons have the parameters that cannot be worked with as they emerge with process and evolution of business. The process has to be worked that would result in the lean making of theories leading to practical elements. A company spending more than 4 hours in meetings cannot claim lean by reducing the costs as it is fake. The productivity

How Lean is Lean

cannot come with the resting or sitting in the meetings. Still some levels need to talk more than others. Where ideas come from have to be in meetings. Where politics come from have to be on desks. Lean is needed on precisely these areas of business politics and business meetings. The employees who need that should be added on to the departments of research or customer relationship management.

Similarly companies sitting on complex technologies not looking at performance leading to lot of defectives cannot be called as lean-oriented. Pruning down on unnecessary business hassles is lean. Whether it is six sigma or black belt or not, lean is reducing any waste. Defect is a waste. Redundancies are waste. Confusion is a waste. Workaholic is a waste. Just as we eat food at different speeds but within a range, employee productivity also falls in a

How Lean is Lean

range. Lean also falls in a range. It cannot hover on the ends of the business fall or rise. An extreme cannot take the company up but it can take it to the abyss. Success does not follow the same ingredient as failure. If failure comes by extremes then don't expect that success should also follow the same recipe. The recipe for business success and failure are different. Lean succeeds only if it can eliminate excess. That is not required for any resource or process. But it stays due to employee myths or managerial imbalances. Some managers cannot let go of a client or process because they have rested their fears or risks there. A single client may be depended upon but the risk is not zero. It is not lean. A successful process is replicated but it does not work beyond a point. It is not lean if you stick to it. Technology is out-dated beyond time; it is extreme in lean because you don't

How Lean is Lean

want to overspend. These are all business lessons that come with time but managers have to be alert all the time. That is lean when you waste no time in digging the roots and causes and effects of errors. Mistakes happen but they have to be corrected in time if adherent to lean. The decisions on the ranges of acceptable process flows and methods to correct them are all part of lean. Here the correction happens first and then the measure. On other methods, we run the methods, observe errors and apply corrections or treatments. In lean it runs to fallacy if the same route is followed. Lean is balanced if the corrections happen first, as it starts from the errors. Next, the lean has to be standardized on the entire process or firm after which the standard methods may be run. There rest not separate lean methods as is nor a different world unlike the common

How Lean is Lean

belief. After the extremes are covered and lean is on use, the business can be as-is. It is like sealing the gaps or cementing the holes to make the normal construction go ahead.

The holes come in when the time is either too long or the material is not good. In the same way, the raw material or process inputs have to be good to make lean. Too much stretch creates stress on companies leading to invisible failures that cannot be covered by lean. Lean becomes inflexible when the managers pull it to extremes as per suiting their goals or career growth options. The options in lean are to eliminate any kind of waste. Hence the offices have developed more work-friendly environments so that seepage is less. Otherwise the companies get nervous about where to take their goals

How Lean is Lean

along with the eccentric employees who dictate market behavior according to their perceptions. A salesmen team declared market as volatile if they cannot interpret user needs well. Another says that is in control if they get the feedback in such manner. Hence the lean is also seen as scissors to cut all corners. But it should cut the middle and not corners. This is where the entire catch lies. Lean measures are the scissors that can cut the middle of the business. But we don't know how to use them and hence cut the most comfortable corners. It is convenience that guides, and that is to be changed in the business. If a manager can cut the corners, then we don't need the lean scissors. The easy part can be done anyway. But it also happens that the employees holding the scissors hold a lot of burden and care. They have to take credit for failure and give to others

How Lean is Lean

for success. After the lean part identification, the lean has to be applied. Not heavy part on corner is really heavy every time. After lean, the company needs to bring back its tailored processes to fit in the whole. The big picture has to be put together otherwise the lean is of no use as it creates gaps in understanding and stitching needs arise for all the employees rather than the one department on the weave.

The lean is not same as the competitive strategy as is commonly thought by most business leads. The action-response is not the crux of lean. The crux of lean is the core of the business and it has to be managed without waiting for response. The witty part of lean is that it converts business into a race with excellence. Racing is possible if the business is prepared on all

How Lean is Lean

grounds like an athlete who is fit on all accounts. The firm has to be firm and ready for take-off on the market without any glitches. Hence the corners that are visible to all can be pointed out with errors. The middle of the business or the interior of business is visible to only few who can handle it and answerable to it. Lean has to be on that to get balanced real results. Any lean or reductions in the name cannot make a business grow if they come along the frills of the business. The company has to grow from where it grows unlean. The non-lean part is what makes it possible for lean and if firms hesitate in facing the harsh facts then the results and growth disappear.

The products have to be good and different. Good is for quality and difference is in innovation. If a product is

How Lean is Lean

out-dated or aligned to some existing success, then it does not copy the same envy to the copying firm. Success does not lead to replication or duplication often. In the given advanced world, it is harder to replicate success because there are multiple opportunities or gaps identified in each product. The scope for improvement is high and the innovation is also needed.

A high-end leap on pruning down the waste in the name of money and resources is restricting the development and not leap near lean. Inputs are always needed for output; the ratio has to be worked by improving the process and investment. Process is for all non-human interventions. Investment includes human side as humans are prone to error and process has to be error-free in order to make the lean effective in the body of the business rather than the peripheries. A

How Lean is Lean

conservative lean also reduces its efficacy pushing the effect to the margins or boundaries. The firms cannot work long with the outside of business entities. They have to come back to the business. The business of companies identifies to be business by coincidence or luck. Hence the resources have to be merged into the business rather than keeping them ashore with the intention of pulling them back whenever the managers wish for. Many firms take out the resources by a short peripheral observation as they don't want to take risk but the real impact arrives after that time of incubation. The lean depends on the incubation and patience thereafter. If a company starts lean then its chances for success are better than if adopts mid-way because it has more open routes than otherwise. It can experiment with options if it has not invested and lost. Business confidence gets hit if lean

How Lean is Lean

is not properly incorporated. I am not telling to buy the tools for lean nor for hiring lean consultants. The firm can do it internally and it is better also as it is aware of the dirt of its employee, operations and machines. Eliminating dust and polishing the business to suit the external eyes gets all attention as we don't otherwise get to merge the reality with the expected. Actual and estimate get together to make lean. a lean business is never a complete business but works in future. It has lot of assumptions, all of them right, and lots of back-up plans, to get them right. Then only lean can become the instrument for efficiency as it is aimed to be. It has to be the tool for business growth by observation and diagnosis of the entities. All subsidiaries have to be managed well to make them function agilely. The agility indicates presence of lean as lean firms are definitely agile

How Lean is Lean

though not all agile firms are necessarily lean. The coping mechanisms with lean lead to border management of the scrapes of costs and such making lean as not effective because nobody can see a picture-perfect lean company. Hence the onus is often heavy on managers who claim lean operations as they are not lean but under the force of lean. the lean has to be shown in the operations without understanding. They adopt last moment measures that are face-saving and hence coping starts with lean. This is not right as lean is meant to be constant. The pressure on lean can be handled with one-off measures but only as sudden trials and not consistently claiming lean. We cannot make the firms run on lean by making them run on toes. The company has to build its strength and growth pillars to run in the market with other companies. Lean companies are thus

How Lean is Lean

not the border guys but internal guys who watch and improve the company prospects. Border guys also have to be lean but with less responsibility only to face sudden attacks from competitors because for them, the corners are easy to attack. If an interior is lean then the attacks on corners can be easily ignored for some time, after which the strike becomes rather noticeable in the market.

Naturalle from USA is seeing the market of lean for the lean people. It is into the business of selling the food snacks in localized markets all over the world adapting to the motto no baked, no fried. It is trying to capture the market on this basis and in the process its business model is also hence wise. It is taking up one market at a time and one product at a time. The product is worked well with

How Lean is Lean

the help of best technologies and ingredients. It does not cull out the short-term benefits by just looking at the brand or needs. It takes the long-term foothold by capturing the market with special only one of its kind products. The traditional food used to be burnt or pan-cooked or such more natural food. The corn and soy are examples which if eaten rawer and less cooked give more proteins. The business model is also on the lean side by making it use more raw materials with low processing making it cost-effective and direct oc item. The packaging is healthy to make it quality sorts in storage and shelf lives. The product is all-machine and only human tested food. The spices and condiments are the fresh ones or with long shelf lives. Then the process is also sturdy in terms of shaping the product and selling it. The chain is thus lean and caters to the segment of consumers instead of

How Lean is Lean

everyone. Whoever wants will pay and it will sell because someone or the other wants it. Compare it with a chip company operation. The lean is only for name here as the firm has to get the real good useable potatoes and other ingredients like oil, spices etc. The process had to clean all and shape up, process further by cooking or frying and then packing. The recipe is like that you may say but the ingredients of corn chips are also similar. Still they render simplicity to the product owing to the simplicity in the operations. Also, lot of chip companies hence have to cross-subsidise with the help of other products because they cannot otherwise prune down the operations. Think of a solar chips company that can conduct 3 operations of washing-cutting-frying in one go and that is innovation. I don't know how that will happen but that has to happen. A two-step process of make

How Lean is Lean

and pack is the future in the lean industry. All else is extremes. In today's business we see a lot of companies working on thousands of processes in the make. They turnaround the unnecessary and claim lean improvements. First of all the steps were unnecessary in the first place. Why should you claim lean for that? Companies have lot of pretext ground that humans work that way and we are prone to err.

Such thing does not apply to machines and today's firms are working with machines more and less with men. The companies cannot judge the machines but machines can judge the men. If a machine is made to work in shifts of 4 per day then that is total lack of supervision. A max of two shifts is acceptable as machines are able to

How Lean is Lean

work in a single shift for 40 hours at a stretch or even 4000 hours at a stretch. We are in 2000s and going to get more into 3000s but not back into powerless recalcitrant days of business from scratch. Lean hence is there today in the business per se. it comes from day one of operations when the CEO thinks twice before increasing the staff from 50 to 10. I would say get all the best stuff into the firm without thinking or else the company will also think before growing. Real lean is to get the best people, best machines and best material without a second thought and then putting them to the best output in the best possible manner. The possible word is very subjective and can trap any manager to save in the days of bad results. Hence she need not use the lean for her benefit. A lot of companies are seen using the lean to their benefit without thinking that using lean is as dangerous

How Lean is Lean

as not using it. Apply lean but don't try to earn out of it as lean is a solution and not a mileage tool. Companies that lose the ground due to excess of defects, waste, resources, wrong decisions, planning etc. have to take the help of lean.

Unfortunately a manager comes to think of lean as saviour of bad business but it can only make the business walk from a sick one. A sick company is so because it has overspent or spent everything well before the time or it has planned wrongly.

The resources that could be utilized for a given input across a long duration to deliver a said output are exhausted much before. The blame goes onto the subordinates or the weak or the smart or the intelligent ones or anybody who cannot conduct politics networking

How Lean is Lean

bosses and self-interests. Any office task is not defined in the book of management in any way that it has to start in a specific order, or then enhanced in a certain way or completed in a given method or measured in a particular way. The measures also are not the strictly defined ones. If your boss claims that your top lines are weak, then you always have the option of arguing for the bottom lines and pointing our weaknesses on top side. Hence the lean does not really help unless the business is conducted with honesty and policy. The saviour of business comes with the leanness over the entire firm's activities and not the external ones. Market may see the business lean but inside may not be so. Then market can easily reflect it in the products of the firm. Customers deny such products. I may set up a firm with 50 people and sell good watches at low price but the

How Lean is Lean

market knows me as lean. The customers can make out the quality if the watches fail to perform after one year. They know the value of money that is give nicely through lean pretext. A real lean firm would sell watches that won't fail for 5 years.

A healthy business can make more out of the existing options by using lean methodologies. There are lot of things that a business is not aware of when it starts. If all that is it ware of is done well, then it can move onto the next set of parameters that grow the firm perfectly consistently. Some companies ignore the first line and move to the second line of improvement. Let's say that the first line is capital, mission, investment, assets, products and customers. The business sets them up correctly and is healthy in 20% margins and other ratios. It is now able to see the hidden factors like market demands and valorisation

How Lean is Lean

needs along with competition. Now the hopes are higher as the expectation is more. The lean here means that the company removes the extra products that it is making excellent but they are not selling. This is coming out of the shell and polarisation to make the company lean. The given product itself may need some tweaking to make it the best in the market. Right timing and correct leaning can make the firm a leader in the market that can pace up before the other players. We cannot see the company as earning money by only going ahead without fixing the gaps. Moving ahead is possible if the company is healthy and lean. Weak companies sometimes need to move ahead to overcome the weakness. The nest of innovation can hide lot of new eggs that can hatch with time but now the firm has to make the best of what it can. The polarisation technique is good

How Lean is Lean

because the company can separate the best and worst of the business operations and products to churn out the leanest of the success. Such success is complete in terms of sustainability, consistency, replication and universal. It beings benefits to all involved in the business and can be used again in the future of the firm. Lean companies can know easily what is in future non-lean so they can work on making themselves healthy to avoid the junk. The junk business decisions that are for trial or ego-related can pull down a business in no time if the leader is not strong. Lean leaders develop by including their vision to fit the needs of the market. A product is neither missed nor forced by them. The junk also lies in the extra resources allocated for risk management that is not existent at all. The junk is in the hour-long meetings that give no meaningful result.

How Lean is Lean

The junk is on the staff that fritters to just understand the machine leaving the rest to machine anyway. We need to support all workers but they are not in the given function, then they have to be put on the fields that they can understand the whole of their life. The junk is also in the effortless cues sought to fill in the sales gaps or the hard-working options that emerge for future but chucked out as not immediately fetching revenues. It is the job of seniors to put the strengths of every worker to the lean.

A lean business can add on to its future opportunities by spreading lean to next lines and resources. Leaders have to take the resources and manage in such a way that half of the future needs are met today. The rest half can be taken care by lean tricks. A business is

How Lean is Lean

already lean, so its managers know how the new resources can be allocated to stay in the same pattern or to improve it for handling future market changes better. This is where the company has to dance from and not from the top of the airs or tips of toes. Business excellence also comes in from top then and not penetrate to the bottom. A business is success if it's lean from top to bottom. The bottom to top lean can also come if the firm works on the internal investment processes and takes it to the outside market. The earnings are made to flow into the sales and volumes intensification. Such firms know the opportunities of future in the same line before others and can finance them ahead to reap the gain on time. Remember that success will come only in its time but we can be prepared ahead on the business level. A firm cannot fight forever for new ideas and

How Lean is Lean

prospects. It can merge or acquire other firms that do not disturb its lean structure or can accommodate the lean improvements. It has to be born lean to be of any use. I am harsh as the birth of company is in our hands so we need to make it lean right from the start. Get the resources and processes right and utilize them wisely to train lean business from the beginning. The employees will also adopt the same model. The value-chain participants will also stick to the model and the lean will be a reiki rather than a dance step. It will be like practise ending never rather than a step for magic business recovery. Lean is itself a recovery of the business growth for its future sustenance and sustainability.

3 – Simple to Practise and Tough to Learn

It is a true statement and also wished for because we don't want to invest our minds in learning something new but to practise something that we already know in may be an innovative way. This is also a key to sustenance and sustainability. Great innovations have come from simple ideas and known methods. Great ideas are known to all of us but we were not attentive enough. The wrist bands for health diagnosis are not a new subject but a new practise. Lean is also like that. It is not easy to teach or learn lean. We have good books and authors but they are the best to crack the toughest practise for us to read. Otherwise lean emerged initially from intuitive practises of Japanese firms. To be honest, the lean is abstract subject but easy practice. It is abstract not because it involves life of a company

How Lean is Lean

but jokes apart, the lean is not defined in any way for any given company. My company may become lean by cutting down the mechanization process routines. Another company may become lean by working on the training of the staff. The lean requirements are very specific and cannot be generalized. The only thing that is generalized is the waste and that is also a very broad term. The polo mints were waste but they converted into the new product and sold as mint crisps.

That took time as initially they were discarded as waste. That was lean at that time. Now people are willing to buy the mints in another shape so they are also lean by selling that otherwise if they sold in initially people would have rejected it saying that is a double-gimmick to sell the waste and core

How Lean is Lean

product. The mission itself was sold on the mint-with-the-hole tag. No book could have defined the lean practise in any way unless the same was practised and found to be successful. If failed, it would have silently left the market and nobody would have said a word. The new shoes that can firm around the feet of members of a family of different sizes are also one of the lean products. You buy one and we sell one. We save in standardization and monetization of the products. The quality is same, price is same, and processes are not varying except for colour. I sell one unisex pair for $500 with reversible sides giving two colours, fitted with soles and fronts that can be closed or opened according to sizes of dad, son, mom, sis or other. What saves on the company are the different machines to fit the sizes, widths, lengths, laces etc. Extend it to multipurpose shoe to get some bottom

How Lean is Lean

fringes or spikes at the slide of a knob on the shoe to make it gum-sole or jogging or jumping or regular shoe. This saves on the company manufacturing routines that form a single process rather than a dozen for different types of shoes. Lean is definitely easier to practise than learn because companies have to finally translate it into their products and they cannot get lean products without lean practices. The lean effort is easier done than said. A company can as is seen in every news article, hire or fire in a day's notice, borrow or acquire machines in a day, add or remove products in a day, take or break vendors in a day, lose or gain clients in a day and many investments are quick. They do not gain much on such accounts but still many are seen doing. If they don't gain then they are not seen doing so often.

How Lean is Lean

Probably, because lean can be attained on such short notices with such quick strategies, that firms believe in the quick games. It is a business idea to start weak and become lean by going for quick fixes. Good games never start and end soon. They pay a good return only if the time invested is adequate in the understanding of other player's moves and doing innovative strategies. Such firms make fresh decisions and new moves that markets appreciate without much risk as they are lean.

Lean companies can quickly adjust to the sudden market changes because they are putting less business at trick. They don't get rigged or tricked neither by the rival moves nor by aggressive events aimed at provoking the firm to make a drastic move ending up as a bankrupt or rejected firm in the market

How Lean is Lean

with wasteful products and investments. The waste is only on two ends, products and investment. If the money invested or forecasts invested are on wrong side then the lean is gone. The firms have to fight the burden of market pressure, customer expectation and intermediary friction along with their internal process complication. The adaption has to come with time as it is not easy. The adaptation of heavy business to lean is not as wasteful as that to the unneeded products. Today all firms understand and do the lean management in all tiers of operations. It is unassuming for the firm to optimize on all products and hence operations. But the product selection is a tough one because it is two-way. Customers have to accept the products. Products have to accommodate the customers. My products are made according to the customer needs but how many

How Lean is Lean

customers can I meet in my lifetime. Hardly any. May be a million if I am luck duck. If I get to read regular blogs, posts, talk in conferences etc. I have to do a lot to get to that many. It is still 0.016% of the total population on the globe.

Approximation on 0.01 % is no less risky than not drowning in a lake. Companies are working on such volatilities. That is market truth and not blamed upon anyone stakeholder of business. How can any business be totally tailored to customer needs in such scenarios? The best the firm can do is to catch a customer and rest all the bets. This is why we become good customer managers or bad portfolio manager. Still the customer today is not a local one as all clients are aware of the worldwide

How Lean is Lean

basket of products and have a global kitty of sellers.

Lean is not a company game but the customer game too. Lean by business cannot be fully lean unless the products are selling lean without piling up the uncaught (unsold + returned) inventories. How can a salesman be taught to run with 1 error per day and get 10 customers on 2 samples? This is ideally lean by theory. But teaching and leaning are different here.

Learning and leaning are also different here. A customer lives in a totally different world from that of a salesman. Books may teach you to get into the shoes of customers but who will let you in? It is also not enough. Let her shoes be hers and your wisdom be yours. Learn to tackle the user volatilities and

How Lean is Lean

you are half done with the lean. When more than half of your business lies outside the company and half of the solution lies outside the company, when is the need for lean to learn rather than practise? Business schools and books all teach the language of the topic in implementation. We have to practise it to get success. Business sees live lean implementations every quarter when it comes up with a new list of innovators or winners in the market for each sector. Learn what they did right and where they did not go wrong to know what lean they put forth in the act. It is simple to see that lean was earned by a firm that cultivated its employees on online trainings not sending them for months on costly program to sabbatical on another nation. The reverse may be true too. A firm is able to get lean as it sent its employees on long-term programs to famous schools rather than firing the

How Lean is Lean

assets. It is a form of lean but depends on the situation. The managers have to take a call as there is no formula for lean. Take a company that drives revenues by employing salesmen on commission. The comm agents bring in money and take a pie. They get a company roll and the firm gets a flexible roll. They can be fired in tough times and they can work on many firms at a time. The gain is two-way and it is lean for both. But this is a very specific case of business and not at all lean formula. The cars companies don't have the option except to be lean. This is lean by default. They have to get the skilled people only and the machines have to make the cars as per the specs to be sold in the market to meet its demand. The supply cannot be excess or less as the product is not a chip or peanut. The buyers are wary of the finance needs and want to buy the best. Hence all

How Lean is Lean

firms strive to sell the best. Still lean is not complete here as the companies are still run by men who are not lean. The firms cannot rule the rooster by making a firm that is lean because the book says so.

They have to satisfy the different parties in business to be on the workable terms. The contracts may be strict but hell breaks loose if dealings of business are strict or lean. Managers have to spend that time and money on clients and prototypes or samples or failures or innovation. The cycles of innovation are seen to be successful with one in hundred. Take the market blog one day and note the number of products flown. Note the products sold next week. See how many live after a month or a year. Most products die within a month of their launch. Others take a year and few last

How Lean is Lean

for years. It is because of the lean that is seen in the product but not in the company. Yeah it happens.

Companies don't realise but they cannot hide the firm from the eyes of the customers. Buyers see a company through its products. A company that heavily underinvests or overinvests is not lean but x-treme. It may sell excellent products attracting and binding the buyers who cannot say no. Such firms are the loss makers in the end and may fizzle out as bankrupt as they buy their own mistakes. The firms that invest in the learning but not in the practical are like the nerds that know all formulae but know not where to use them. They fail in the simple tests as they don't tell which formula to use. Men or women have to think business before going lean. The main cause of failing lean is

How Lean is Lean

because it is seen as theory and that has to be mastered first. It has to be mastered first but in the hands not in the brain.

The managers have to administer it to machines or desks. Tell the people not to waste time in passing tests on TQM. And they will most probably implement it because they see the business daily. Tell them to use lean and they will make its application instead of groping for the statistics and formulae. They know that he or she can do one's task better than others'. The task has to be put to the leading of output. Even if output does not come as well-executed task is half success. A well-started task is half-done. A lean task is half started, and does not need much to be done. Even if you give books, they will do what they can. Thus the understanding has to

How Lean is Lean

come in the doing. Workers don't learn to do but they do and learn. Lean also has to be done to learn. It has to be practised with lot of attention to detail. True. Not many stand up to that. We all want magic formulae to apply to any situation for better results. But the best results come only in one way. Be aware of all business scenarios and weaknesses. Alacrity is needed in business to be agile. Agility is needed to be lean. A firm that practices things on lean grounds only challenges itself if it does not have the full background of the gaps and ups. The managers of the new shoe company are working on lean because they do not overstuff the inventories. Still they don't fire the extras but put them up on innovation. Anyway the firms don't have all people with degree-job as one-to-one match. Anybody can do anything once on hire. They don't complicate processes with

How Lean is Lean

over-inventive methods. It is a simple modification of the old shoe.

That way manager is able to see only the slight change without seeing a new complex shoe. The managers told that they can get outsourcing at a lower rate but they want to give the best quality and hence using in-house staff on small tasks by paying them high. The low returns of course made them to relook at the model to convert into outsourcing model in the short-run so that more volumes can take the help of internal staffs. The volumes are also not forced on the market. There is less advertising because the new innovations die easily due to intensive ad that covers the potent of the product. There are not many sources of purchase because the public feedback is first needed to launch it on multiple sites. Success backing the

How Lean is Lean

accessibility is much more long-lived than the reverse for the business. Over discussion or over availability may kill the speciality of the product making it a common one without any buyers. It may also make it prone to rival barging or masking as buyers to only kill the product. This is also lean for the company that earns lot of future business opportunities in the market by making it as demand-generating rather than pushed product. Dairy Milk Bubble is one product that has made a funny step-in. It has come out of a huge customer survey but pushed by a manager's idea claimed as customer's. The product is not able to see demand but is pushed in the market because the idea was innovative and different more than innovative from other products or chocolates in the market. Kitkat also launched with similar idea but boomeranged. Now it is settled with the

How Lean is Lean

masses. When ideas are not so favourable to public but cannot be killed because of the groundswell generated, they have to be tested for some time to fathom other's needs and plans. Or that is the company belief to even divert from the news of chocolates being infested and defective. Food is a sensitive sector and any deviation can land it in the pits of masses.

Certainly it is not lean as the company is only waiting for debacle to happen before calling off its mistakes, then it won't be in the race of lean. It is following the book and not act. The operations team is working on the only possibility of luck working in favour of the product one day when all others are despised by the buyer. Or because it is not harming the health of buyers it can stay. Well thought but not favourable to

How Lean is Lean

lean business if it has to break the barriers of success locally and globally. A lean company has to become lean if not necessitated by the market conditions. Market conditions are hence volatile because they create room for every working business. Whether hard or smart work counts and business survives. Success comes only to the lean firms that act smartly but work hard. Quick decisions and intelligent business strategies along with intensive research, surveys, conversations with market accomplices are possible only in lean companies as otherwise they muddle the whole business with lot of data. Data is good but not always. Sometimes we have to work lean. As said above, we cannot get the complete data anyway because we cannot work with the entire customer set. Half knowledge is more dangerous than no knowledge. Learning lean is anyway not

How Lean is Lean

a formula so it is better to be with it rather than sorting it in the mind. Be rational with your business partners and mend your employee ways. You are half lean. Get away with the market excuses and false pretexts of using methods because you like them personally or your boss feels good. Those who could go against the bosses are the ones who succeeded in lean. Lean does not mean deviation. Hence I prove that it cannot be theorized. Bosses are right and they have to be followed but only when they are for it for the company. Their personal hunches may be right too because after all a business is found on personal hunch rather than service or book recommendation. I do flowers business because I like the business and my passion lies there to make flowers of all types, real, fake, paper, cloth or plastic. I won't donate the lots as that is service. That is once in a while

How Lean is Lean

acting but not a business act unless it is NGO. The lean also works in the same way as it is for the business growth, not for profits or sustenance. The profits can come through several routes. The business can sustain anyway. But growth comes only with success. And vice versa... the nations worked on people and companies to grow. Today companies follow the same model.

They work with people and resources to grow. What else can we do when all else comes out to be standard with all firms ready to do everything it takes for a winner? Lean does not make winners but eliminates losers. Lean makes the path to winners. It is a route to winning in the business world without compromising on sustainability and profits. Can we win without the two? Wal-mart. GE. The first one has no

How Lean is Lean

profits but growing since decades. The latter has no sustainability with scores of portfolios because one could not sustain ever but growing on the whole for decades. Take the other way. Dell has profits but not growing like HP or Microsoft. Winning on all accounts is rare. Citibank is winning, with profits and sustainability, growing on all fronts. It has recently cut down its branches like Wal-Mart but both are on different lean paths. JPMorgan has sustainability but no growth. Even with all the acquisitions the companies can do one or many things in business but not lean.

Leaning is to make the business fit on all aides. Customers should not say no to the products. Investors should not refuse the new ideas. Intermediaries should not pester for better margins. Suppliers should not yearn for deals.

How Lean is Lean

The companies try to cut down loss-making operations with the help of lean practises. It is also difficult to fathom the necessity of business if not lean. Everything seems to be important and hence the non-lean becomes fat or unsustainable. There are millions of companies making profits but that does not mean that a company doing all of that would necessarily make millions in profits or even sustain for sure or that a company has to do all of that to make profits in the market. They worked their combinations of lean well and each company has its own success combination that cannot be procured from outside. The lean is also visible in the same results but found in different forms. Some common statistics were identified as harmful to lean like the clichéd costs, staff, old machines, routines etc. But the lean has to be found for each company based on its

How Lean is Lean

success ration and business. The discs company cannot become lean like a pen company. Pen needs more men than discs. Pens have to be written and tested by men while discs can be tested by machines. We don't record ourselves on discs while we write with our own hands. The company can cut lean on different parameters. Freed of the unused resources or oft-occurring defects or the excess raw material/ inventories/ end-goods, or unwarranted bureaucracy a firm can boast of being lean and attract all the market observant. A company can then kill its flaws to show a healthy company en route to success for making others to join or follow. The more the adherents of a path the more chances of success. Business needs innovation with one firm making a difference by adopting a unique path and creating entry barriers making it a tough business sector.

How Lean is Lean

Profits and success go to such firms but the situation is not of a business that competes by staying in the competition. It is like a competition with no competitors. Future is going to eliminate all such finesse for the lucky businessmen to grab it once in a while. Hence being lean is the only competitive yardstick making it a tough ground for business of tomorrow. A lean business can be smart. A hard-working business can be lean. Or a business that consumes fewer resources can be lean but it takes a lot to be lean.

How Lean is Lean

4 – Where not to be Lean

It takes nothing not to be lean. Let's identify some of the comfort areas for the business. It is important to know where not to be lean simply because removing the business resources from key areas can end the KSF (key success factors). The firms that conserve on resources to use them when needed are doing favour to them but it is not needed. The advance investment is not a real wise thing to do. The commitment of resources to future business is ok to a small extent. Companies must know where not to keep lean. The places are important for business to fluff as otherwise the competitors get no worse places for attack. When rivals compete against the increasing research and innovation it creates a situation of healthy co-growth. It is a win-win situation for both. If they

How Lean is Lean

attack the basic products not letting the firm retain customers, then one loses and the other firm wins. Also if the firm reduces its innovation only to make lean so that the other rivals also don't compete against interventions then that lean is harmful to all the players. It stands against the rules of competition and is not beneficial but malignant competition. Also where the companies cut lean is where no expenses are involved. They allow non-lean if there is not money. That is wrong. Don't cut the profits but cut anything. Running behind profits cannot create a sustainable business. Same is the case with customers. Adding them endlessly cannot create the business sustenance. If there are expenses they have to be lean. In fact, if costs are left to the non-lean then company can grow without any worries. The business suppliers and cost centres operate on automated

How Lean is Lean

transparent structures with no scope for waste or prowling. Once this is understood, they can get to the next step of improving the lean lot. Of course small companies start with personal relations and negotiations with vendors as they must keep a watch on their employees to avoid leakage or plundering. It also opens up door to the next level where trusted suppliers can be relied for best pricing. Hence with time, non-lean should be applied to the places exactly where lean was applied earlier. This is intrinsic to all firms that they find the lean places to make them non-lean as otherwise they tend to convert into problem-areas for the business. This is the first step to identifying the non-lean areas. Firms must not be lean where they have been lean for more than 5 years. It however does not answer the defects past. If a company has not produced defects for

How Lean is Lean

the last 5 years, it can relax because its operations have evolved to remain the same. It wont reverse the policies anyway as even if it finds the foes for its products it can always buy on the defect free quality. The lean is not anymore applicable as the area is lean already. This is the second area or a sub-area of the first. Next are the customers. No lens must be used here. Non-lean and lean must not be used here and hence by default non-lean applies to customers.

Employees must not be restricted in the way they satisfy them whether with extra samples or returns or credits or exchanges or offers, a new thing can be worked at any time for any customer. The freedom rests with time and not with subordinate or manager. It has been seen that companies lose opportunities in the time the reps take nod from their managers or bosses or as they don't want to lose the job. If a customer is offered a go no worker must be punished for using the company resources. A step has to be taken ahead to please customers if the facing agent feels so. He or she may be naïve to offer extra help but that helps the customer to be aware that the employees of the company are aware of all their stakes and involvement. As at the end of the day, the company belongs to employees more than the customers. The extra help may be in a gift or explanation or error on part of the customer herself. A lot of customers are seen to be friendly with the staff on stores and they even remember the birthdays to send them a gift card etc. When a famous kids' apparel company told a complaining customer that it is not their responsibility to provide noise-free

How Lean is Lean

but hygienic blanket, the mother came rolling in laughter the next time that her baby was playing with the only friendly quilt at home letting her work in peace. She even gifted the rep with a gift card after writing a letter of appreciation for the company.

That is the type of response that customers give if their mistakes are tightly and rightly pointed out. A second instance is by a car company when the buyer threatened to complain about the salesman giving a faulty car. She took it and got it repaired for a fee but forwarded the mistake identified as the customer's when she gave it to her minor son who dashed it against a wall. The customer later agreed that she had to be careful in getting the wheel propelled by proper hands. The same company also got a valid complaint

How Lean is Lean

when another customer got a car that broke on the next week of purchase.

They repaired it for fee again that the maintenance was needed in service station. The buyer got some accessories for being faced with the need so early in on the purchase. The buyer also took umbrage and sent the complaint to the heads that made sure that the car functioned without a problem for the next slot of 6 months or one year. A car has to be serviced in the start and periodically, but not before that. The owner was happy that the car didn't break down for the next 5 years and he got a good price for selling it. This is the type of service that does not look at nothing but stores in lean. The customers have to be given the full right to know their faults and get the reversals. When the car company got

How Lean is Lean

the next service need, they gave a free one to reward the customer once. This is a goodwill gesture and firms must appreciate that their customers are foregoing a lot of other options in the market, not all of them worse but best ones even, by going for the given company.

There are times when buyers give up better options and go after a buy because of family choice or personal preferences or time factor or age factor. Letting high on a company's staff or technologies is non-lean and sometimes only good for the companies. Forgetting the name of the company is making it lean by leaps and bounds. Not adding too much weight to the brand and name gives a company tremendous freedom to work with the customers and experiments. Apple can never launch a

How Lean is Lean

device in the mass market though its customers are even students. It can never capture the largest market by reducing its prices or products in the slashed segment. Is it not possible when Staxx can sell $4 phones? The name is hypothetical and masked. Apple is prone to sell $400 phones or devices because it has positioned and identifies products by that. In a way it is moving away from lean. Definitely, brand is needed, no doubt. But non-lean can be made here. Firms don't lose for a while if customers use their products without signifying the brand. When a premium entity sold a product in low price every user suspected to be low quality and did not buy. When Blackberry lost its market share it urgently launched a low-end phone but masses took it because it was a reactive timely move. Now the firm makes sure that it creates a cheap phone with every hi-end sale. A $100

How Lean is Lean

phone comes in the market as a $500 phone is also launched. Of course market has forced the firm to take up the strategy as a survival one and not out of a passion for satisfying the low-end customers. It is a lean-by-kneel. Otherwise the company cannot sell the phones only on the basis of a specialised network, personalised OS and customised apps. Not all companies can be Microsoft. A firm has to accept that it is lean even when it compromises its lean but goes for lean for customers. Another area for cipher non-lean is the product innovation. The cycles may be long but the features may be in still development. Vexed firms leave it to market to decide the product cycles by its success or failure. It is imperative as otherwise also the same is going to happen. Keep innovating and leave the rest to product. If it incorporate the new features, then it is adaptive otherwise it

How Lean is Lean

is in need of improvement or it may be saturated. The companies cannot win on the basis of low innovation as users don't know about it. But it is needed for pushing the buyers to the next level. Far perspectives come only with long leaps in innovation. Lean innovation can make the companies lean by profits and growth.

Innovation can be in any area but more importantly in products as they outweigh other outputs of the company. Only products sell and they reflect all other lean so they must be lean also. Other things that companies can sell or 'desell' should also be noted though not for money. The brand, goodwill, social acts, public favours, quality, employee ethics, firm integrity, corporate equity do sell or desell a company's image. The levy should not be on money but firms do

How Lean is Lean

include it in price as that is wrong. If they become price then people do not carry the trust and loyalty coming in the package as return gifts. You never return a paid gift. Shares were also initially not bought for bucks. They were issued as partnerships or bills like gift vouchers or extra product or other form by companies but not as paid stocks. Later people came to ask for a paid certificate as that would make high-involvement and not free, but credible authority like other founders in the company. Therefore it was mentioned in specific that they have no voting or veto rights. If it's free we don't feel like the owners but if it is paid for we get the rights and play. They were restricted to some close players and not to all general public at large. Money as a measure is easy to quantify the returns and investment. Lean was adopted where it was seen to fit and not where it

How Lean is Lean

was easy. Today we know it by monetary gains or losses but earlier it was purely based on the business functions. There were no recording, documentation, assignment, bifurcation, allocation and trending. When the business ran out of intuitive limits the lean was applied and it worked in most cases. There is no need to be lean when the company gets to the desired levels of growth. Then the inputs and application have to be in full to ensure the steam for future growth of business. The growth may be with the help of technologies but it can never be automated as the market conditions can never be controlled or saved constant.

The regions where products are sold and demanded are ignored and not related. They are seen as demand creation and sales gaps. However the fact is that companies are unknowingly applying lean here when it is not

How Lean is Lean

needed. The companies sell because they want to sell in a region as they see the projections for customers. The regions where demand exists are where customers want companies to sell and not because the products are creative. The need is there and hence must be met. But companies use tactics of pull and push to make their brand felt. This restricts free sales and movement of brand in fact. The company gets to retain the hold in places where it wants and not where it is wanted. There are also fears to not disappoint buyers where they put in demand. The products are verified by firms to meet all standards.

It is not necessary for companies to be lean every here and there. There are times when firms need not be lean like at the time of product introductions,

How Lean is Lean

market entry or exit, press events, promotions and uneventful times; they are those when the company comes across a sudden setback from the customers or others in the market, or a scandal is nailed out. The firm has to forget business and be the defender. It has to offer the solutions to the offenders and give a redress. It has to be performing like the man and not an entity. Men would protect them from dangers, and firms must also. The manager in position should take the help of the offenders to understand what their preferred mode of reclaim is. The groups of opponents had to be merged when Canada Dry faced dry in the back times. IT was the decision to be not in the non-lean but they came out. Companies don't stick out their nocturnal eyes in the day normally but they have to when the markets bite the nose. How can a company claim to be

How Lean is Lean

lean when its founding tactics are in question? The soft drinks firm owned up the fault not actually theirs and admitted that they had to improve the quality of their drinks. They took to the market after making a new drink and got the good sales out of the new drink. Today the soft drinks space is ruled by few who are into the fizz and formula. Hence is known as F-sector instead of cold drinks to distinguish from juices and non-soda beverages. The lean companies tend to be constantly lean unless told to stop. The consistent leanness is not again good for the firms that have differing customer presence and varying market trends.

Depending on the possible share, revenues, growth, input-output ratio, companies ought not to be lean in the number-centric areas. Numbers form

How Lean is Lean

due to the activities of the firm and they have toes of the lines of the business to run on. Letting them run is ok as the competitors are watching. Cutting those makes rivals wary and they also dig back into the details. The satirical announcements come when one player copies another or gives a decision only in response to others rather than creating good avenues for the firm. Where markets can go violent, firms need not be lean and where competitors go wild, companies should not be lean. Nokia consistently got lean as competitors responded wildly. It should not have gone lean on its costs with rivals finally throwing it out of the market.

Samsung has not gone lean and is still there among bad times too. Markets find the stiff in the bad times and they should

How Lean is Lean

be able to bend enough to customise to the changes by not being lean. It does not mean that if a firm is not lean then it will find its way easily among others. It has to still create its cold waves and tough voice through clarifying its stands on the products and competition. Grilling itself and others would help the company sail out of the unfavourable times.

The areas where companies need not be lean are the indirect expenses, free investments, cold-calling, frozen rates, piratical shifts and heavy opposition. The communication is one area where firms tend to be lean to avoid the arguments or criticism.

They don't want to lead the markets in different directions, nor want to provide it with lot of data about their firms. But

How Lean is Lean

this is again wrong. Giving data and information about the firm makes it easy for the company to let others think for its next steps. The vendors and competitors are able to judge the firm and its ventures. The firms that act in secrecy succeed fewer times than the open ones. The big firms find it tough to stop being lean because they start at a later stage. They end up non-lean by cutting down everything into lean. They are so much into it that they don't realize that a big company like Remington need not have sold its units or cut down its machineries. It could sell machines so it had to be non-lean but nobody told it to so be.

When companies go into hibernation or events both are times to be non-lean. The period of inactivity should not be culled with more inactivity. The firms should hire more people, go against the tide to buy more machines and build

How Lean is Lean

more products. They should hold themselves in the business cycles for continuous performance rather than growth. It is an effort for growth but they get to grow with the market when it allows the differential growth to the firm. Differential growth comes with the normal business cycle followed during abnormal times. The firms know that they would go for the event of growth only after the market becomes normal, naturally and rightfully. Sometimes markets remain in abnormal times and show out to be normal but the business continuity can help then though after real markets perform. When companies underperform, they should not be lean unlike the popular belief. Bad firms cut down on the business cycles when they want to save on profits. Good firms don't do that. When they fail, they take up the lean to non-lean to take through the business in a non-restricting manner.

How Lean is Lean

When Lehman cut down its costs after a poor quarter, it closed down itself as the leaning killed the company. The rough quarters cannot but ail the firm and so it has to sail by not stopping. A typical firm of 5 years old, with more than 1000 employees has to spend at least $1 b in one country's operations each year. If it does not then it has no business prospects because a billion dollar-expense covers the business from troughs, risks, fights, brand-dulling, employee-stagnation and outdating. The firm can then gain the ground of excellence and growth without much leverage on the old investments that would be disturbed otherwise. A firm growing in all time is one that manages between lean and non-lean in different times. A firm not yearning for growth is one that leaps between lean to leaner to leanest. A ship sailing in the water becomes lean if it does not do anything

How Lean is Lean

but sits idle in the storm, and then ticks the risk of sinking also in the waters. The cost of company also becomes low if it does not do anything but it is again lean that is not lean.

Hence it is better to be non-lean in such times. The good companies become great when they don't save on unnecessary places. They save where it is not but wasteful. A firm gives all preference to the employees who work for the full day but ignore the ones who work for half day and achieve more. That again is not lean but erratically lean. More time is not good time, more work is good time. When less time gives more output then that is lean; when less input gives more output then that is also lean.

Getting companies to lean takes non-lean and the importance of not to be

How Lean is Lean

lean comes here. Let the companies survive on the name of the long-lasting ties with customers and quality rather than small lean achievements like small size and easy costs.

When a new branch is located for a firm, non-lean applies as any reduction without full skills on the area is risky of losing worthy deals. When a new employee is hired, non-lean is needed as to give her the best offer to get her in without betting her with other rivals.

As a company transitions from one growth phase to another, it should be non-lean to account for unexpected change in the market. A good growth comes with the discrete decision as per the market situation. A firm may grow or

How Lean is Lean

stop growing according to the market but more as per the unneeded lean or non-lean structures. A big company or a small company has to follow non-lean without amiss. A small firm has to run by the norms of growth, big firm has to fight to alter it. A small firm can fight non-lean; a big firm has to be non-lean. Firms can understand the market signals also if they non-lean at times or else it sees no room for lean.

In a company teams learn to adopt lean as rote for success in the times of business even if good or bad. Teams should be taught to adopt non-lean for the same success in good or bad times. If a manager finds that a firm is not able to take new people and hence not able to take new projects, then she should not go for lean; she should raise the brows to show the necessity for non-lean against lean. Tiny resource sizes, team sizes, project sizes also make the

How Lean is Lean

firm tiny. Non-lean approach is meant for the companies that want to avoid the unwarranted tiny growth. It is also a part of the firm transition to know when to be lean and when not. It takes time and free-associating to not be lean. Firms must go for conferences and meet others to know the trends of lean in the market. Often when market does not advocate lean, it is best staying back as otherwise the lean may backfire at the growth.

How Lean is Lean

5 - Leakages in Lean

The firms are all on the tread for making their companies lean by passion and fashion. Companies must try to adhere to lean to avoid the unwarranted wastages. But often companies start leaking during lean as the trimmed down costs crack to reveal the poor quality or as the thin staffs melt the payroll to reveal the unskilled workforce or the companies themselves cant sometimes compete with the new risers and innovators in the sector. The emergence of the companies to increasingly grow by lean is lacking in the foresight or hindsight on the long direction ahead. The saturated markets cannot grow if companies stop taking irksome risks by putting a stop on the non-lean or by forcing lean beyond ages. The stringent lean makes the tasks inefficient and slow. It makes the staff negligent. It

How Lean is Lean

converts growth into stagnation. Many companies have seen that when they continue with lean without paying attention to holes, leakages start in the company. The business falters with customers and goals. The savings go into unprofitable ventures that heed not to the customers but to the book of making 0 or 1 in the market. The binary lean makes it difficult to try different segments and products in the market thus making the company devoid of the lean benefits. The lean in waste, defects and risk leads to more waste, more defectives, adding more risk. The companies become non-lean to cover the leakages but the intermittent rise of costs does not make the leaking firm any hep in the sector. The staff dissatisfaction is half of the leakage cause in lean. The low employee strength cannot accept the low pay, and low career progression with low visibility

How Lean is Lean

leading to customer walk-outs and client walk-aways. This results in business slowdown with the take-aways of lean vs. non-lean pointing out the entire blame on everything except lean and the reasons tend out to be the lack of data, weak skills, anorexic business appetite, revealing strategic points, unstructured business models and grinding hours of office. All these also are the results of the lean that is not monitored properly or implemented properly. The firms don't get to spend time on lean but go on pacing with lean. This is the point of leakage. When also the firms don't intervene in the competitors' decisions by not sharing their views, the lean stinks as their acts are totally out of sync with rivals'. There are times when companies benefit a lot with the use of lean like adding to the efficiencies and improving the performance. But equally prevalent are

How Lean is Lean

times when companies lose out on the customers, due to tight CRM policies, and they may even lose their brand due to strict brand-promotion activity. The effect is to get the firms out of the turmoil by providing a quick first-aid followed by reprisal. The companies also have to go for redresses. A key innovation may be totally missed out in the hectic time-to-cost competition matching. A product may be defective by function though not per se. Motorola was the first one to adopt six-sigma but it came out with a model that itself was defective when it launched the cell phones, hence it rolled the model back for corrections and got it right the next time.

Hence leakages can make the buyers ignore the defectless piece. They are not always lean what go through lean.

How Lean is Lean

The excess resources gone into the mending of the lean projects create non-lean results slowing the growth of business but they can be overcome soon after the coverage of leakages. Good companies try to prevent the leakages by sending the lean processes for testing to other companies like vendors or partners. A lens of third-party can cover the gaps of lean in any company for if it works fine in another firm then it has to be working fine here too with minor changes. Normally lean can be tested within the firm but it is better to fit it into known models for checking the results. It is better to be fool-proof than sensitive. The lean cannot be reused but a leak-proof model can emerge out of the combinations of lean by mixing two-three models from different companies. Known firms are like the suppliers, vendors, subsidiaries, partners and clients. Often we use the

How Lean is Lean

client-tailored models to run away with the losses and the leakages. Lean is too critical and hence it leaks as the implementers are not aware of the simple and some of the aligning items for business. A simple re-routing prevents and settles the leakages of lean to growth.

A simple courier company closing its branches had realigned the tasks to handle more efficiently per day. The losses bled and then stopped giving the firm a health and profit. They has removed the staff as lean measure, again a wrong one but still valid because the founder did not have enough to invest and marginalise. He then went to the airlines and worked on a deal to get the flights on a cheaper slot for 2 hours every day. The packages were re-routed for delivery at

How Lean is Lean

a given time if received before a deadline daily. There was thus a two-step courier process unlike the big ones who have multi-step processes.

The firm did not have problems in dealing with off-peak hours of cargo flights as they were able to get them delivered by the extra staff at destinations. The firm cooled off the leakages and gained edge to continue the business close to shut-down.

When new companies adopt lean, they are also likely to show excesses, because the lean is unplanned and random. The model does get accepted and new clients team up. Resources have to be built and work needs to start on such projects to avoid the delays. The start goes well but slows down with time and growth. The staff are the ones who are skilled not able to handle other

How Lean is Lean

generic works. Then the benches cannot be made to work on multiple tasks. This is a lean leakage.

When there are nuances of business leading to unexpected changes or unrealistic expectations, then the firms cannot close on the lean commitments or when the company stretches goals beyond the saturation point, the lean leakages are bound to happen. And the non-lean happens when and where not needed. The companies get to build the capabilities in such a way that they are able to get maximum efficiencies out of minimum inputs for maximum projects. The time, effort, resources, men, machines, and output are so aligned that a well-performing firm gets the most out of the least. That is lean as it converts the waste into taste. The success for the business lies in the

How Lean is Lean

ability to pull out the growth magic by the given time. After that it is too lean or non-lean with leakages and before would be on the inefficiency side. The trained members can take and levy lean where needed, to avoid the losses or leakages from the business growth parameters. The companies create a lot of goal based on the lean. This also leads to leakage when not backed by the proper tools for bridging the inefficiencies and customer relations. When a firm entitles itself to lean it thinks that it can easily handle any market owing to its ability to give output at zero-defect and most optimum level. But the outside reality shows difference.

The customers and markets give varied feedback leading to the company's clash and rift in confusion and delegation. The employees tend to

How Lean is Lean

ignore the mission and just make it work. It leads to borderline targets and output that is lacking in standards. The health of the brand gets affected and so the company gets excess losses and less profit. The firm is not best suited to adopt lean and gives up lean. This creates an aftermath leading to unidentified losses, ineffective policies and untraceable customer shifts. The meagre presence of the company in its market makes it look lean but by leakage and not growth. Lean by growth is without any leakage. When company grows with customers, internal skills and markets, its lean does not lead to any sort of excesses or inefficiencies. Everything in the market boils down to productivity and yield. A firm hence becomes a machine adhering to that. The firm does not let any errors creep into their processes or avoids all losses by man-made, like the controllable risk.

How Lean is Lean

Then the lean without the leakage gives growth. Hence it is true in both ways. The run from lean to growth is bi-directional and can be achieved from the inputs that tend to protect the output and vice-versa. The outputs also seek less input for processes that are lean. Hence lean is a weak term if not accompanies with tight, straight, orderly and timely. The business has to be tight in its utilization of capabilities, straight with its goals for customers or market, orderly in its approach with competitors and internal sponsors as well as timely with the market and product innovation. The importance of research cannot be overlooked here because a firm exercises surveys and study throughout its existence. The company growth depends on the internal data more than the external or big data. This has been proved and debated at timeless times that the details that managers get from

How Lean is Lean

customers are more precious than the big data from machines or statistics. The stores, factories, outlets, and other points of sale are the incubators of small data as they interact with the customers directly. Coke encourages customer visits to its factory because it wants them to learn how it manufactures the fine drinks using the hygienic ingredients, flawless processes, expert technologies and clean packaging. Now the customers have no source for mistake or wrong information about the firm if something goes wrong, they can also visualise and trace the source of mistake. The news on a drink being not original is out of question as all the bottling happens within the premises. Any news about the water being unhealthy is not credible as the water is provided from the source of municipal dispensation. It shows how the firm is eliminating the need for and cause for

How Lean is Lean

worry to the customer. There is no scope for lean getting leaked anywhere. The entire process takes less than a minute to make a bottle of Coke and hence lean by all means. And in the tasting factory, there is no lean as it allows all visitors to drink as many cups of as many varieties of more than hundred there of beverages in tea, coffee, juices, non-aerated and flavoured drinks. The aerated drinks firm has thus diverted its lean leakages to new products and multiple brands. If only we think of any lean discrepancies where the formula got leaked out of the locker placed in the central hall or that the machinery was dirty or the packaging was flawed, then the company would not have been able to launch so many varieties as it 'ld 've lost the market confidence and also it could have focused its resources on the solving of the existing issues instead of

How Lean is Lean

expanding to other lines. Same is true of all successful companies that either averted failure or learnt from the failure to reap success in future. How many of you get to learn from failures? Many. But we rarely do. The grease of machinery can decide how much of the lean is leaking. It is that easy to make out. It is blatant. Firms cannot cover the leaks nor hide them if they don't get to know about them. Often, market notices a leak before a company. Managers are so immersed with the tasks whether one or more, in their own speeds that they don't get to see the internal flaws. Their inefficiencies guide the company growth and they rule the volatilities in the market with equal participation.

Riverdale firm, a famous one, sent its Director for a business deal worth $4b to a client in Aeronautics. He was

How Lean is Lean

restricted to the outer factory premises and he signed the deal in the conference hall. A Managing Director was present from the other side. The firms were working on a business intelligence and data crunching project for utilizing the latest tools in gaining the business insights for tracking the budgets of different centres. The lean project was aimed at re-channelling the profits to the new areas like AI and NCs. The project took off and the results were dependent on all the processes and operations of the firm based out of more than 10 locations. The communication was not proper as the employees had email access and the notification was sent only to the heads. They were requested to keep the numbers masked. The first futile attempt in lean led to leakage of the tender bids. The next failure was at the product level. The budgets were constrained and the

How Lean is Lean

managers resorted to puppetry or fact-twisting for getting the output. The quality couldn't suffer as they were based on previous standards and client specifications. But the leakage occurred in terms of the excess costs being covered through stretch or scope-extensions. The client was upset leading to next contracts being passed on to the new firms. This is how modern firms will gain ground due to fault of others rather than excellence of theirs. The next futility was along the value-chain, where the third-party or outsourcing teams came in. They were not informed but they got to know from the outside. The employees' attrition rate rose who bore the mistrust factor from the firm. They moved to other firms from the senior levels which is the most difficult to replace and hunt.

How Lean is Lean

The head-hunters had to be hired paying in for the excess hiring fee. The competitors got free bunch of hot cakes without a fee. The alerts were sent at each stage and the firm adopted remedial measures but the lean leakages had happened by then. The company could recover to some extent by bringing back some of its past employees offering an unnatural hike amidst the natural disaster. The lean leakage was also on the front where the firm hailed the communication and called on all employees to inform them oddly about the failure. It was late by then…too late. The employees cursed, laughed, some did not undertake a reaction as they were ignorant of the whole concept. There were series of training sessions, investments and re-assignments of projects with reshuffling of managers.

How Lean is Lean

The analytics teams wanted to inform other teams of the finding. Meetings were held and finally the trends and data were crunched to the benefit of the companies and customers involved in the entire business of planes.

However, the lean got to be appearing as a magic demon that can either enhance or hamper the projects. This is due to the ineffectiveness of staff and the firm got to accept that soon as the external consultants would never take the blame for the faults of their clients. That is how the business is running. If the vendor took some blame then that would have removed the blemish from the concept at least to make them work in future.

When the theme is put in red by the vendors for fear of loss of face, then the

How Lean is Lean

business takes a beating through the market. The other players also feel the same as all are human workers. They are all emotional and find default blamed. It takes another vendor to convince or another concept to buy the client. This is again wrong as the vendor also should have ensured the aversion of the issues by being on the emails or premises be it just the meeting room. As much precautionary scenarios as the vendor could provide, it helps the client so much in avoiding the failures. Customers should not be allowed to blame concepts but people of the vendor or client. Then the things can be better otherwise who can expect a concept to defend itself?

The lean would be a leakage itself if it does not get absorbed in the company operations and activities. It should not

How Lean is Lean

be executed like a separate project for one or two years like any other assignment waiting to be over. Companies and managers have to be tactful because lean can never get over. It starts with the company and continues through its growth. If lean is made to start and end like a switch, then company is bound to see leakages. Leakages can be in costs, quality, skills, ethics, emotions etc. Employee emotions get awry when lean is viewed as a trick or short-term gimmick. Managers try finding a template for lean to fix dates and rates. But that sounds loss-making. You don't want your company to treat a way of success as a temporary measure. The firms often make the mistake of stopping lean in the middle when they feel things are going wrong because of their faults but cannot admit them for fear of losing promotions. In such scenarios, the top managers

How Lean is Lean

smut the firm with task-failure or weak foundation. But any company is founded on solid principles because starting is always exciting and it involves few words and dreams. The founders are more ambitious than the temporary employees.

But the companies must struggle to find a route to amalgamate the lean functioning in their routines and processes. The employees ought to be made to adhere to the lean principles of not wasting time, effort and money. This basic line can prevent any leakage of firm finances or customers or ethics or rules. Even competitors are told about secret strategies when employees are not aware of the lean. They think that it is one of the painful points that their bosses are putting them through and reveal to rivals the same. Rivals are not

How Lean is Lean

going to take it light. They would implement lean with better results and ease.

The pricing can be more efficient due to lean and rivals would create the impact. All this leads to more leakage of lean within the firm. They may not be able to tweak the lean in proper places to make it work. Adjust lean on people, stock and time points. Reduce all deadlines deliberately by pushing them backward. Employees have to work when they get multiple deadlines. They would finish the same work and can do same earlier also. It's just what we allow in stretches, whether time or effort. Let the stocks be compact and in-time; cut all the stocks to get the best results. Excess stocks only create more leakages or outflows. These don't go to the customers but to the garbage trucks or dump-bins. When

How Lean is Lean

firms are not careful of their stocks, they commit to wrong segments at wrong times as customers don't mind shifting to others for a short-term creating mirages of market shares but handling none to the firms in reality when they show their loyalty to the old company products. They may not even tell their friends to buy.

How Lean is Lean

6 – Lean Improvements

A company never adopts an approach without the intention of improvements. Lean also leads to improvements in the business as it starts on a rough ground like a raw tree, there are lot of areas to be cleaned and trimmed to make the firm grow with healthy consistent results. Lean gives the healing power to business to cure its defects and make it healthy for further growth. A firm gets to learn a lot in lean. It comes to know how timely internal tasks help in matching market timing. It gets the art of leading its company out of the weaknesses and makes others follow it. Market following is helpful in recognizing a brand and guiding innovation in the winning front. When a lot many companies follow a single firm's innovation path then the new products tend to be competitive and encouraging for the customers. Otherwise the customers find their own products that may not be really on the same sector. For example, customers

How Lean is Lean

found calculator in their phones and the other sector took a fall due to that change in the segmentation with a new or different product. Lean improvements create defined slots and spaces in company where the new market challenges fit in to get solutions or the new needs find a place to get firm into the growth phase. As industry grows, it creates equal spaces for all companies putting the nation into a path of opportunities. But only few companies can retain them because they use the new chances to cover their old flaws or adjust in the wrong market growth goals. The companies can adopt lean and improve their business acumen as like any other profession; business is also more based on intuition because there is no book to tell steps for starting and growing business. The firms have to make their decisions and opt for the right strategy in a given market condition. This does not happen correct in most cases. Few companies are lucky to get it right. Few are smart to get it right.

How Lean is Lean

Careful planning and lean improvements can give the company time to wait for the right opportunity to occur in the market. Mostly, firms are not able to wait because they face pressure from the competitors or customers or other value-chain members to speed up a decision or go for inaccurate market transitions. The business transformation happens in a wrong way leading to future non-lean, flaws, and failures in the company or as slow growth and inefficiencies in the company. Companies get swathed in the rivals' directions because they want to compete and get the surprise gifts in the market not knowing they would get only the flawed gifts in that manner. Firms that analyse well and act as per the market conditions, get to make fresh moves with a new scope for growth and innovation avoiding others to copy that unique model.. this is possible only through lean as otherwise the firm does not understand its own potential truly

How Lean is Lean

well to tap it or sustain it. In the olden days, business houses used to take a decision after a long-time but that time went in deliberating and careful analysis. But today, we only put off a decision for some time without doing much.

This is artificial leaning and not the healthy business lean. It does not lead to improvements hence and can only make the business temporarily lean upfront and non-lean behind. The internal or interior structures cannot cope with the improvements. When lean is not proper, the outward enhancements cannot be absorbed in the firm and this is another major talk for concern. The changes for good create shocks or jerks in the business growth leading to hiccups and slowing of the business progress. The perfections create doubts and fears among employees, percolating up to the top leadership levels that ignore the benefits flowing down from lean but focus on

How Lean is Lean

overcoming the new obstacles that are merely nothing more than illusions. These cover the lean and make non-lean from inside. Anything that comes from inside had more impact on the business than if from our markets. The external impacts are easy to handle but not the internal ones. A firm cannot focus on lean if its employees are busy solving non-existent or self-created issues.

These concerns lead to loss of revenues and such monetary losses should be give importance rather than the ones helping in regular conduct of business. The gaining role of lean is hence to open up the business to be clear from inside so that when the external environment offers a new set of growth leads, the firm can bank on them without a major restating or restructuring of business. Lean puts up a lot of bricks for the positions needed for new growth or extensions or expansion of business. The business is not a road to

How Lean is Lean

follow but a structure to develop and walk along the path of customers. It has to vary according to market demands and not remain stable like a stone. It has to be light enough to move along innovation and strong enough to sustain the challenges of market. Lean improvements initiate the tension within the different levers of an organisation to make it move as per the required speed in a given direction without losing much time on internal transitions or external transformations. Firms have to fulfil the external change initiated on the internal structure to be able to take full advantage of the lean. But the technologies, manpower or inventories have to be upgraded or updated if the market demands so, and even this can be brought out in lean. As part of the improvement, lean makes everything clear and open for the company to work and employees are motivated to complete them because they are able to see the fruits of growth as clearly too in lean. The customer growth is visible, the new market potential

How Lean is Lean

is known, the possible earnings are accurately estimated and the new product success can also be envisaged with equal skill.

The lean areas are the strong areas because they have the flexibility to add or remove the new opportunities. Sometimes, business does not necessitate new growth. It has to be put off for a time and waited for the right market conditions. New products and solutions often undergo this wait period but this is lean period with better growth scope if followed under lean operations. Otherwise it is like any other growth zone to be followed with inputs to get certain output. The firms cannot repair the weaknesses not can reap the complete set of gains in revenues and customers. Then the value-addition is not realistic but a game to the market. The value comes with the price and goes with the customer. The sustainability is not lean but forced and that creates non-lean inefficiencies or

How Lean is Lean

non-lean dynamics. The effect continues to last over the coming transitions and business growth falls low on the skewed side. A symmetric business growth is preferable and comes only with appropriate lean implementation. The cost-reductions flow in, and the company revenues too rise, along with the skilled forces, in men and machines. The company also gets right kind of raw material and quality can subsist. It happens without much doing.

When lean subsists, business growth subsists and the company subsists on a growth level. The phases of business get to a better level of progress. Firms can go to be higher on their stakeholder value than if without lean. Without lean does not mean that the firm will be totally the opposite of lean, some changes do come with the firm like lean but they are not noticed or miss out on the right perspective. This affects the future business decisions making the firm

How Lean is Lean

dependent on market corrections and rival reactions. The managers lose competency and tend to be more reactive than alert on the internal strengths that develop without much effort when market recognizes a good move by a company. The statistics of a company's growth depend not on the numbers but on the capabilities of today and tomorrow's business. They become growth transformers for the company and conductors of excellence in the firms. The size and age of the company then attribute progress in the exact proportion to make the firm reliable in the market with the correct relaying of the communication signals from and to the market interventionists. The analysts then look at the company as a leader rather than dormant onlooker acting upon the crucial market signals only. Companies must act on the crucial signals to revive their growth losses. But firms that also create signals by their positive growth activities can become superior to others. The firms in such growth trajectories are called superb

How Lean is Lean

business entities. The black belts and six sigma are hardly of any suitability if the company itself is failing in the basics. The basics are not referring to high school fundamentals but the basic ingredients of mission, rules of operations, goals of firm, skills of staff and approach to market.

Lean drills down the improvements to all levels right from top and bottom. It can percolate to any level or plane of business growth.

Don't look at it as a quality only approach. It is to tone down your business to get the mark on the market. It levels further crests and troughs generated in the business by market or internal triggers of entrainment. It makes the business market-friendly by introducing the improvements that are inherent in a firm. Such changes don't need additional investment and can increase the returns. This is only a

How Lean is Lean

benchmark and not to be worked for. If a firm works for money, then it is bound to lose. If a firm works for improvement then it is bound to win. If a firm then moves to the next level and works for customers, then it is bound to become a leader. Then if a firm works on the next level for innovation, it is bound to become value-adder and market giant for it has the support of customers and employees. How many times do we take a relook at our work from the point of view of understanding its mitigation of inefficiencies, importance to goals and value-addition to others? Only in appraisals, and rarely so because we tend to influence our seniors with the personal strengths or unneeded achievements rather than the core ones related directly to the business… first, the managers should remove the school methods because the grading routes rest the enthusiasm needed in workplace. An office does not need jesters or competitors but involvers. The work has to be down tied to hectic deadlines and methods but not to scores or

How Lean is Lean

points. It is not a book test but a live test on job that has different ways for success but not a single formula like 1 or 0. 10 or 100 marks don't make sense because the same problem can be solved in a different way leading to varied output in a bank or a mobile firm or a good firm or a goods firm. The firms mentioned here can still be tied to many other sectors and hence the worker should be free to grapple with the areas of the business to give full results. Managers tie definite goals to avoid deluding by employees but the good employees lose out since managers being highly human tend to ignore the extra intangible brought by the top employees of the firm. Either they should become top by numbers or they should create a movement in the market to be recognized. This happens by all means only in the end. Tested employees are those that don't excel by marks but by means. As a top scorer in college I don't have a problem in getting full marks from my boss but the other workers who get results better than I

How Lean is Lean

would debilitate in their morale and confidence.

Also, it allows for flexibility in approach otherwise every worker tends to work with the marks and numbers obstructing the customer management as the areas that are not goal-centric would then be left to wait for leaders to create standards. Such gimmicks are only for consultants who want to create change in the firm but the change is not for the firm. It is for a department only. The whole firm gains if employees are awarded motivation or prizes to grow further with training or experience in new skills and concepts. Moving an employee to a new project can add more value than forcing her to achieve 10% more numbers in the same stagnating project. Lean helps employees do everything of this sort.

How Lean is Lean

Controlling expenses or raising revenues or inflated balance sheets cannot put a company on lean growth. They should come on their own and in such nuanced way that the progress should not be visible internal but external. The market must mark the changes in the upward direction. The managers even if they don't see the growth can strive for more thus making lean more pertinent on the business direction. This is where the real HR function comes into play recognizing the employee contribution, to growth. Again it is the next level of excellence and a company is hardly able to take their HR to this level except in the top few. Even the top ones focus on core areas of hiring and firing. Only the most brilliant companies get to the stage where their HR becomes the goal-seeker and not the goal-provider for highly innovative companies. In many contexts, right and wrong, people feel that product companies are the only innovative ones but that is wrong, as services firms can be more innovative if not less. Yes,

How Lean is Lean

that is a fact and services syndicates can get more scope for innovation by structure, operations, design, strategy, focus and pricing in lean. Lean structures are those that generate gains in reporting and project management. Lean operations bring gains in costs and pricing.

Lean designs beget gains in customer value and delight. Lean strategies gain in high-end financial status, market position and brand recognition. Lean focus enhances gains in export, import, and knowledge and employee retention. Lean pricing bring in gains of competitor bargain and global market accommodation.

Competitor bargaining is the time and scope for reacting and acting against competitors despite their aggressive tight moves to restrict the firm or market growth. Global market accommodation is the flexibility in redirecting market efforts to the

How Lean is Lean

firm growth or making them favourable to the customer enhancement. Pricing is the end of the tail where the customer pricks the firm most. Protecting it can give the firm a better rattling capability to shift innovation in different directions otherwise innovation is not a job in isolation. Most firms think that they can make any great product and the customers will accept it ultimately because of the strength of their research but we don't bother as customers what you do in the company. You as a buyer want to fit the product to your need and mood. Yes, that is true and buyer psychology guides firms to adopt to the moods of customers when they come for shopping and when they can appreciate the features. That is why shops are closed in the nights because the brains also shut down mostly during that time though the customers may be awake. Lean improvements help gauging all the customer moods and tranquilities to place the products or redresses at the right time and composition. Even complaints that

How Lean is Lean

may be addressed best by the firm can be ignored for more fine-tuning like products or services if pestering customers feel that the company can be troubled with more stringent demands. Sometimes like all others customers can also be annoying and there is a full need to retain composure as firms can hurt their prospects only in such times if they don't show their qualities of management, relationship, flattery and allegiance. Lean not only enables the customer handling but also uncovers that when we expect from a customer loyalty, retention and brand recall, we should first have those ourselves in our employees and promoters. The ads, products and ethics should reflect everything that we expect from the customers. Otherwise we can't have it from them too.

If a firm is ignorant of its strengths, then market cannot be expected to be aware of it for sure. It can be recognized but as a chance. If a firm cannot flatter its

How Lean is Lean

customers, it cannot expect its customers to gain flattery in its products. These are extra things and one also tends to agree when managers say that their business is different from these. But if done, the firm can rest into future for centuries to come with success. Lean gives the scope for directing the progress along that direction of giving something more than the business.

More is always liked by the market if it is in the future progress direction. Direction can be dictated by the markets and customers retain more weight in the task. The activity of retaining customers is possible if the firm is able to retain its best employees. Business growth is a chain effect as one change percolates similar impact on other constituents of the value-chain. The business cannot grow if the customers are left to the mercy of products alone. Managers have to interact with them though customers may not prefer any

How Lean is Lean

undue interference of the company reps. And still at the end of the quarter, they tend to appreciate the true interventions aimed at solving the customer problems. They may not respond to emails for months nor attend phone calls. But real customer servicing would visit them or send free samples or new products without expecting the money or escaping on the pretext of the customers not accessible or available to their reps when such firms only create happy customers by turning the disgruntled ones into favourable and favourite. The tall program labelled black belt and other trainings can help the managers assess the lean improvements better but hail in the limited direction as the books are always with formulae and not offer open scopes for growth of business. They apply to certain areas of business and managers hesitate in extending them to new ones. Books cannot be challenged. So it is better to learn the concepts and implement the management concepts to attain the full business benefits to the firm. Japanese

How Lean is Lean

firms are known to excel at these because their culture in personal and work areas is strict with strong ethics. They wake up early, sleep early, eat healthy, respect others, ignore weak clients and envisage improvements in all spheres social, political and economic. Business is viewed as a progress sector itself and not a commercial practice. The investments are tuned to get the value-additions rather than the returns. Where companies view value-addition as the end-result, revenues and profits accrue along with customers. When firms view profits and end-result, then value- addition has to be forced like customers who have to be pulled and searched as they don't come on their own. The companies take to taking the business essentials and not the losses. Losses are individual firm's results of business knack or lack. Business per se is the collective activity with value, customers, losses, gains, products, potential, technologies, employees, society and community rest on the business together. Lean improvements derail the

How Lean is Lean

losses and stagnation to make the firm active in its participation with customers and stakeholders to bring about a positive change in the community. This is the reverse of the business cycle that sees bad initiatives throwing successful entities into losses. The reversal is the preferred mode of business response and lean can get that. When firms seek knowledge they don't apply it directly to business because they don't want to experiment but that is not trialling, it is the to-do really. The firms have to adhere to the principles of books to make sure that deviations are not letting the flaws creep into the applications. However, most companies today customize even the book theories to their company practices to make them more relevant to the growth and operations of the entity in internal and external entirety. Lean monitors the growth identifying the gaps to fill in the new success parameters for the company. Hence we should strive to make lean work for the company rather

How Lean is Lean

than wait for the company to work for lean in the uncontrollable situations.

7 - Why Lean is only not Lean

Lean cannot be lean when the company goals are misaligned or misjudged. Often, the companies expect that hiring lean consultants can get their firm become lean. But becoming lean is not always lean in the firm. The firm becomes lean but it is still not lean. This has to be understood because the misinterpretation of lean as explained above leads to wrong expectations from lean. A lean company is hardly lean as its numbers are still more on the higher side and the costs too as the company gets lean in the paper but not on the operations.

The employees are inefficient and the tasks are not fully in line with the product functions. That allows for creep age and lot of extra work adding no

How Lean is Lean

value to the business flows. The workers always find the blame with others and they deviate from the norms. The top echelons only try to balance the internal unrest and ignore the much needed to solve market difficulties. The managers get to work overtime for money but not personal or business growth.

Lean is everything but lean. The staff numbers are not low but on the expanding side. The goals are ever-increasing and the investments are going all ways outside and inside a country. The national growth is elevating from lean industries and the industrial growth is stemming from the economy. The relation is important as retaliation of market in the lean direction comes from that. Companies adopt lean and monitor market response to adjust their goals

How Lean is Lean

and systems. The result is the change in the lean output and the impact falls on the economy. The cumulative effect of lean in firms and industries and the markets lands on the computed growth rate of economy. The productivity and efficiency enhance the growth of economy and industry together as lean growth is not reversible. It brings definite progress and development if lean is not judged but followed in the business. Repeat lean improvements in the firms to get growth of economy by getting vast progress in the industry sector. When firms expect a tight line of developments then lean is able to deify another line by shifting to business in another direction. It brings in a combination of unknown growth factors leading to the business upheaval if not interpreted well yet the lean gets firms on a new track of growth away from the strange market deviations and stifles. Lean is tied with

How Lean is Lean

sigma or belt to make it more relevant to the business times and it is not for confusing the lean definition. Lean is meant to trim down the business to optimise the utilization. This is the aim of any business in any sector. Tie this with economy and it is the aim of any nation to grow in a definite direction by managing the existing capabilities and increasing the productivity. The inefficiency and yield of the nation is directly related to that of the industries and the growth rates of industries are directly dependent on that of the firms. The unit level of influence is at the customer or product entity. The product can pull the growth and the customer can push the growth to girth of firms. Many firms want to wake up to a morning of magical growth in a news article or exchange movement but that is a small constituent of the growth.

How Lean is Lean

Growth of a business = growth of firm + growth in market + growth in rivals +/- growth of exchanges + growth in technologies + growth of staff + growth of products + growth in innovation + growth in customers + growth of economy

The growth of firm is the direct numerical composite measure.

The growth in market is the scope offered by the market. Ignore the gaps as they won't harm the firm unless the firm uses for undue gains. The growth in rivals can make you grow by copying, competing or participating in joint ventures. The growth of exchanges creates a downfall or upside in the firm's related development. The growth in a related or unrelated industry also makes a difference to that of the firm's. The

How Lean is Lean

only way the lean can be applied and known is by measuring its partial gains to the intermittent flows of business. The entire business model is complicated for any company. A lean gain may be visible in another unrelated operation but it flowed from lean. That has to be known and praised for managers to believe and trust in lean. Otherwise lean does not appear where expected or desired. The lean may affect the indirect flow or unrelated chain bringing in the best operational gains to the business.

The lean business is not something like a pencil or a knife that is sharp and slim. It cannot quantify and show as lean as hoped for by the firms in all times; the lean may become non-lean in some measure, and leanest at others. The companies get to measure the lean business not by the results on the top

How Lean is Lean

lines or bottom lines but on the liens in true sense. The cash flows get more reliable and worthy of earning interests or worthy investments. The number of managers involved in lean is isolated from other projects thus making lean not lean. The number of projects on lean itself is large making it the differentiated methodology not same system as business.

Business is lean and lean is business. This attitude should be adopted to govern the lean methodologies to get them in the commerce and industry development in sync with the regular operations. Lean as a single term has got so much recognition because it is tough to master. It is like run, conduct or growing. Of course the terms are not as easy to adopt as others. Business depends on the aggregate of a wide

How Lean is Lean

range of parameters to gain success in the world. Growth does not come with the rise of two quarters or gain in revenues for a decade. Even a century of business sales is not good enough for growth. Growth comes by the value addition done to the other segments of business in customers, products or community. The first one is direct for which a business is commenced. The second one shows some extra innovation on part of the company from the industry side. The community growth is the last on which the business growth rests by growing the trust of non-customers also in the process. The alignment of business interests and the involvement of all the participants of the larger ecosystem give a growth that can be hardly diminished by competition or volatilised by the market. The firm gets the finest growth that is dynamic and rapid to lean changes voted in the

How Lean is Lean

market. The company does not become lean on its own but by adopting the latest improvements and operating on a daily scale to match the customer needs. The newest technologies cannot save the company if it does not look at the balancing of and managing for the business lean.

The quality is often seen as the only go-getter when all else fails in the business. The lean can be non-lean even in quality. We expect the defects to be zero but the dynamic programming can constantly create error in the output. That is not lean but it is in the direction. The lean may come in with separate girding of the limits and ranges in the low or high levels of the acceptable and unacceptable divergences. Leaning on lean may only be not lean. And companies have to accept the truth as

How Lean is Lean

early as possible to reap the full gains of the business growth. Often firms wrestle with their resources in making men work and machines graft towards making a successful business. Work can get success but the business is winning for the market and customers especially. The competitors have to be defeated because they try to give a better deal to the customers. The defeat had to be by best customer service earlier, but no way today, as it is more to do with kindling competition to collaborate in the market rather than beating them by winning their customers. It's a mix and acceptable if the market is so calm. Unless volatilities drive the business, the firms are going to find the easy way out to make the business survive by cartelising rather than hard route of appeasing the customers. The customers cannot win if the companies don't work for them. The companies

How Lean is Lean

cannot win if the buyers don't let them work towards their interests. Customers have also got to work for the companies but by making them get to the ground of the best business. Yes, customers can make them be the best business by looking at the intricate business matters with a lean eye. It gives scope for future improvement as the business gets to work with customers and dealers together. A product firm can see it easily in terms of turnovers and sales. A services firm can see it in terms of productivity and clients. Employees and customers are assets of services firms while products and sales are seeds of product firms. If the grouping is not clear then firms tend to mix up the goals and targets from cross-industry or cross-border parameters leading to lean stepping out of lean. Lean can be anything except lean in successful times also and companies must understand

How Lean is Lean

this in order to be able to appreciate lean. The weaknesses of companies get hired in non-lean inefficiencies and the strengths also get multiplied if firms know that lean is not that lean. The non-lean is easy to see and remedy. The strengths can become multi-tasked weaknesses if the lean is not recorded and progressed to the next path of business growth. A lot of companies make the business wander in multiple directions by acquiring unrelated firms and expanding to new lines by banking on the venture capitalists' or others' confidence. But a single unit runs on its own and takes market help. The founders help the business only to the extent of making it firm on its founding principles but no other experience of theirs gets the business on a growth trajectory except the business itself. For that, it has to become lean and agile. This is a simple thing and normal

How Lean is Lean

statement but a business takes decades to get it reflected in its growth. A business may grow in time and size but not in its business. A business grows in its business if it is lean. This is like saying that a core of the business should also grow with time to make it a real growth. The core of the business lies in the central theme of octagonal principles, mission, vision, charter, market, product, customers, and seminal technologies.

This entire spectrum has to grow to lean to make the core lean to make the business grow lean. The principles of business need rumpus by discussions and redefinitions to make them relevant and modern. The same old values can and must be repackaged to get new ones to be followed by the new generations of hierarchies. A manager

How Lean is Lean

may find it boring to be called truthful but she may be excited to be known as rule-abiding. The mission and vision are old but they have to be rephrased and reframed to make them look relevant to the times and evolutionary phases of the changing and expanding companies. The firms don't get to change if they don't make the participants understand the value of change. The charter can be redefined once in a medium term to align the goals to the interests of the customers. The products have to be grown to grow the core by adopting latest innovation and customer feedback. The customers have to be grown in personal and purchase domains as otherwise they cannot appreciate the growth of business in the long-run and down the next generations. The market had to be respected earlier and today it has to be grown by the business renovations and progression.

How Lean is Lean

The core then grows to healthy business also with the growth of key know-hows on which the corporate was originated. This encompasses more than the required range of business participants to make the growth of the internal business a feasible activity in the long-run. This also covers the lean in such detail that gains and losses all lead together aimed at growth of the corporate advancement. Secondly, lean also combines a lot of progress variables besides lean. Lean is not just lean but lean and clean. A business has to adopt the straight practices to get itself running in the market. By standards, bureaucracies and rules, it has to grow up to be able to get gains. Lean gives the ability to be clean. Lean is also to make business wean non-growth. The business is in a position to wean itself from the effects of competitive digressions and narrow

How Lean is Lean

short-term measures. Unethical and illegal practices must be weaned. Lean is not making the business lean only but mean also. A business has to mean customers, products and service. It is not selfish or narrow but focused and developing. It gives meaning to the business to be more affective of market changes to the gain of the society. Such business growth is again lean and dean. The firm acts as a dean of all the companies in the given unrelated or related industries where it connects with its business growth. The union of lean and bean is another starting point for new businesses that can evolve along with the next lines of business ideas and fruition indications opened up by the lean spaces. Next is that company tending to gather a lot of strengths with becoming lean? Hence it is for the overall business health that lean is important and not just few indicators.

How Lean is Lean

Business becomes at times, more agile and profitable than it is expected. There are the positive times when growth comes from the real gains in customers, markets, products, and internal corporate growth. The lean is not lean but lean to the core. The potential to grow increases the headcount, investments, expenses on the company turnovers, fast innovation accepting defects to make them a stepping stone for the next flawless innovation. That becomes a blue ocean churning out new products and methods for the sector thus taking the sector to the next level in the development. Such innovation is the need of the next century business and lean is going to make it possible. Where we look for new business scope comes from such innovation that rolls out multiple products and gaps. Each gap comes with a new weakness and solution with a new strength to

How Lean is Lean

encourage markets demand stringently different products that make the firms cut for breaking innovation. Lean innovation is the exact precise product that is offered to the customers and they don't refuse it but buy it. The next line of business is built on a new line of products along those lines so that the innovation gives rise to the lean in the next line to make it perfect for the business. Lean thus pushes lean for the next business era.

8 - The Lean Line

The lean border is important for companies to derive and follow so as to avoid the overflow or lack of lean results. An overflow of lean, results in time mis-variances with nothing in the future. It brings in excess growth leaving

How Lean is Lean

the future free of the good scope. Lack of lean results comes due to under importance or neglecting the real business parameters. That is why the above-mentioned alerts have to be managed in not getting finicky about the costs or leakages. Such things are only distractors and cannot help the long-term growth of business. The line of the lean falls along those parameters of business that affect the short-term and long-term decisions about expansion, product-withdrawals, technology, up-gradation, machinery, acquisitions and ad-spends. Lean does affect ads also to a great extent. The marketing and promotion of the companies gets affected to the worst taking the back seat or extra attention than needed if the lean makes a jump up or down in terms of the business parameters of costs, staff, skills, tools, mission, with market response and internal methods also

How Lean is Lean

making a difference to the firm's progress. The path of lean business is simple and the line has some major factors.

The factors may not vary but very minor way if the firms feel that a factor really needs work or replacement. Mainly they fall along the line looking at the acquisition, creation and management of customers, markets, shareholders, investors, technologies and other allied things like partners, nations, geographies, etc. that aid in enhancing the scope of the business or the operations. The companies cannot run from market realities and have to make plans to be lean on the parameters that may gain hold at that time or stay heavy on the palates of the sectors. Still, lean line has to be uniform and not curvy or topsy-turvy or haphazard. The line

How Lean is Lean

cannot put costs and profits along with the innovation because innovation needs a boneless investment and lower costs may result from innovation but innovation cannot result from low costs. A firm that lowers cost cannot expect the innovation run from there, I have to hire new resources or engage the current ones into the right kind of innovation backed by research and capabilities. My firm has to own the machines and tools to make the innovation possible. Only knowing the idea or conversion is not enough, the new product has only to be produced by the firm and made to be used by the customers or prospects before being accepted as innovation. The lean helped earlier in identifying whether a company was light enough to be capable of the entry into new segments or new business ways. The portfolio or market or product or methodology has to fit into

How Lean is Lean

the lean to be big enough to make a difference to the business. The business if not lean already would reject such ideas that may suit only lean firms. It may not be blatantly visible but that is bound to happen. Market will say – no that firm cannot work on the new idea... the firm cannot take up the new lot of business ... as the firm is not lean ... or they have excesses in staff or costs or deficits therein, of skills also or the cases as analysed show that there is more than 50% buffer in every firm on the resources- both men and others. Workers are not ready to accept this truth because then they would have to be fired.

Companies cannot accept the truth because they well prefer to mean oversized than undersized. The CEO keeps her mind free from daily rattle

How Lean is Lean

because she wants to engage others in the tasks. The others want to engage still others and the chain goes up to five levels in each task. The efficiency is hence lower by 50%. Works gets done in the same time with double the staff. The truth can be accepted and then the firms need not remove the bench but rotate them neatly into the innovative tasks or operational improvements or lean to be precise. The line has to be formed with the help of lean staff and lean methods with the lean hierarchy clear. The lean is totally for the business progression and the reporting should be not in terms of bosses but task achievement. A manager has to report to his subordinate if a defect rate is reduced to make him aware of the next steps. A junior has to report to the head about the change in the yield not to impress him bit to raise his pay but to track the ranges for future and profits

How Lean is Lean

accruing to the firm out of such measures. The lien can take on the business operations to shed it or add to it by freeing from defects or increasing the worth value. The lean line can therefore put itself on the aperture of deficiency and defects, taking forth on the path of perfections and advances in the business.

Some employees are bound to stay on either side of the line as some are able to claim the change on positive side with others complaining about the lacunae on the other side. The effort should be to pull the other side to this lean way to make the firm functional in all aspects. The investment on new fronts gets evaluated in terms of NPV and returns but the key thing that gets missed out in the firms is their lean. The lean is seen as some new item that starts after the

How Lean is Lean

business is mid-way on transition. This is a wrong notion or a myth in the business minds that goes for a change today in the name of technology.

But technology cannot make it happen if managers don't drive a change. Lean though is not a change is so today because of the wrong conceptualization or illusion that it is a different method or new pill of health. It should not wait for the disease, as it is an energizer or revitaliser. Even before, it's an ingredient of business without which the firm cannot cook success in the market let alone boost up the fillip. Firms then really need to cook up success without much market or customer followership, but basing merely on the investor fame, brand value, dealer strength, and network of stakeholders, prevalence of skills or man-years and college brand

How Lean is Lean

name of the workers or founders. This is a narrow success; it has to be changed totally to face the customers and the markets. Customers are the front and the markets are the back of the business face. It gets effaced with the mistake of not going lean but going blind in the market to gain the customers. In such context the aim of customer acquisition gets profit or money-oriented. Business then suddenly suffers to the worst.

Immediately, firms look towards help from the unknown sectors of mergers, customers, distributors to weave a magic on the business front. The new business initiatives fail because the lean that was missing earlier now works to show its absence in the new areas. The yesteryears went in business getting itself busy with the traditional tenets of ethics and integrity. Today again we go the modern tenets of lean and growth although both the sets are dependent on each other. Ethics and integrity lead to lean and growth. Lean and growth are not possible without ethics or integrity.

Lean is not separate from growth because a lean entity can identify and do a lot of business initiatives. Lean growth is the most preferred mode of business development. Development by lean leads to growth without fail. Growth does not lead to lean always. Growth simply means that the business entity is not shaping up but only enhancing the firm in certain upward directions as detailed out in the book *Business Management in the 22nd Century*. The growth tends not only in the linear, upwards, direction but movements, downwards at different speeds in a static area. That is to say when a firm is not planning for any expansion but in

How Lean is Lean

the same portfolio adds some customers, removes some products, rise-and-fall trends, varying the reactions to market demands, unifying the competitor reaction and internal capabilities to make the firm move instead of remaining inert. The fashion of lean business is in since beginning but companies prefer to get deviated by many other things than lean as it is wantonly easy to handle the unknown than do straight for the business. You can blame it on a boss for not giving you the budget or the juniors for not attaining the skills, why you missed out on the target given or expected; but it is tough to say that your goal got missed due to the customers rejecting your product or tough to do a regular client-meeting to rope in their support or partnership for the growth of the business.

How Lean is Lean

Firms don't grow because they adopt a technology or run behind customers. They grow because they do that in time or attain the efficiencies to safeguard the company from tough times as what firms do to save them buys them confidence than achieving straight results however great that may be.

The great firms are those that earned time to think through crisis and got the leader standing through the prosperous times of the industry or economy. Lean line places companies on a test of the company grit to make them realize where they stand in reality. On the business ground the firms make losses for not sticking to the mission or for trying to exceed the line. The line is balanced to imbibe the needed and remove the unneeded. The low side is the need to be wise in getting firm to

How Lean is Lean

lean side by allocations of resources in the optimum and efficient levels.

The high side is the exceeding of the firms in overdoing their optimization so as to fret the resources draining the efficiencies to a little extent. But this line could have saved them from a future debacle. The leaders' cane makes the workers run towards efficiency and their absence makes them move away from the failure. A company looks up to its leaders to lead the path to success as business growth finally means career growth of its contributors. Employees, vendors, clients all promote employees of any of the three grow in any way due to the attempts on the customers delight path. The skills are not enough just as the experience alone does not suffice without the added degree to the higher leadership level to become credible and

How Lean is Lean

authentic. The real leaders make the lean effective by making it non-lean while implementing it initially, later pruning the methodology too. They give full freedom to the managers and invest heavily in the lean to start it so that the employees don't work under stereotypes limiting their tasks to desk or progress report. The bonus check or the full-score card does not lead to the long-term growth of business or the contributor. Contributors to business are all the employees, dealers, vendors, consultants, distributors, customers all try to make the company progress in several ways and directions.

The activities are not limited to the few top ones or key ones but lean makes every activity significant and important to higher echelons of the business. The subsidiaries and the companies involved

How Lean is Lean

in the organization create lean to make the entire line lean. It is a composite make and not a simple one to be lean.

The complexities that lie under the making of lean make it lean and therefore eliminate the further complications from the business. A firm's liable to face all the convolutions of business but they wont further confound the growing. The intricacies of the business can only be simplified with the lean. The densities of business issues rise or fall with or without lean. The firms can make or break the profits but for lean. Lean fixes the direct outcomes at different periods of time in the various forms of profits, expansions, customers, added sales or growing employees. A company gain a lot when the resources are productive and not idle. Similarly it does lose a lot if the

How Lean is Lean

productive resources are chucked out of the business. Bidding on the best price, busying firm in skill reformation, buying on the best fresh material to give the best outcome whether food or non-food, electronic or non, service or product, the lean helped and would continue to. Hiring lean or not is not an issue but adopting or not is. The firms not going lean are not non-adopters but poor followers of lean. A company mandated exercise for all its employees to create a culture of lean in its organization. The small firm in Latin America mandated the presence of its workers in the gym for 30 minutes per day, though this is a deviation but in the right sense. The time that the employees put on the job anyway goes out in various other breaks and outings. One form is to consolidate some of them into working out lean on the premise that lean employees would know the worth of lean. Even if they are

How Lean is Lean

done with the role, their involvement creates the culture of lean in the firm. Though it's a remote relation, a rather inverse correlation yet, the company gained in its lean operations when the teams showed similar commitment to the goals in using of lean.

The line of staff working along lean entered into the world of lean without much difficulty. They did not have boggles of mugging or certifying in lean as they wanted to work on them like in their bodies. The bodies of staff became well-affluent on the lean whether for their bodies or that of firms. The men worked on the lean in terms of operations streamlining, or skills moulding for activities, or the levelling of the real vs. expected results, happened through leaning on lens of lean. The line marks the beginning, end and toggling

How Lean is Lean

on lean. The firms stand on the lean and jump over or upon the lean line to get the best results of lean by standing to the maintenance of the elements of the lean or playing with the constituents of lean to get different amounts of lean. Lean can be controlled to the extent of procuring the lean benefits in small packets or proportions as needed by the firm or expected by the top management.

When old companies would talk about conservatism or single focus, the new day firms send them off as traditional and not the right fit to today's business. They find it more appealing to find the solutions in a new form for the same old problems of the business. The new order firms fetch business based on the

How Lean is Lean

modern day principles that sound like expansion and liberalism but they hound the company to the same old goals of snowballing revenues, or sales, contracting losses or costs or they get to sides like stock raises or price-lifts. The firms adopt the same old lean to get the modern lean to make the firm modern in context. The objectives and meaning remain the same as earlier when they say that a cut in the expenses is needed or that a new product is needed to reorganise the portfolio. The form of user involvement is either minimized or bloated according to the state of business in the market, whether it is close to bankruptcy or on the approach of uptake.

The lean is hence also getting more or less due to it based on the meeting of the business with market reality. The more it is in market terms, the more the business is lean and vice versa. The less the firm is prone to change or adaptable to market volatilities, the difficulties get accumulated in the user deliverables, and the firm suffers due to the corpulence in the daily operations tarried due to the non-lean structures. The line of lean hence combines the worlds of lean, risk management and volatility assessment to make the business function better than ever. Each progressive year of business brings a new challenge and lean enable the firms in identifying the problems correctly so that the right solution is applied without delay or extra cost. This is also the dear wish of business houses and founders. Go with the sincere adoption of lean to give it a best sheen. The saviour of good business and annihilator of poor practices along with nurturing of all growth parameters that make the firm

How Lean is Lean

serve the customers is the lean need of the hour.

The firms can get here with earmarked focus on lean and knowledge on the lean successes should be passed on to the next teams in all departments for easy emulations and simulations. The business is only doing a favour to itself by adopting lean in its standards not limited to the routines or operations. The hiring, quality, production, testing, manufacturing, sales, distribution can all go lean for the best aftermath in business conditions of all sorts as thrown by the market. Let the firms evolve with markets by adopting lean in their goals of daily or periodic growth. Lean is the well-wisher for companies, by giving not only the required space to grow but also the path to learning while appreciating the world of business. The

How Lean is Lean

managers tend to work only for the pay and fear only the loss of pay. This mentality does not create the vivacious workers to pay the company through their value-adding efforts but they wrongly put their effort in other's jobs or waste theirs in the name of lacunae from the firm's side. They don't try when faced with the situation, but only leave the project, change firm or crib to the rib. This one works only when true volatilities bind the firm out of all access paths to roaring success. Otherwise the employees only bring down the performance or efficiency of the companies. The intention of the company is to combine the top-line goals with bottom-line deliverables to the stakeholders. Lean can combine the top-line with customers' expectations to match directly with the Board's goals. This takes a lot of work in terms of understanding and translating user

How Lean is Lean

needs to the corporate goals related to innovation and strategy but not just revenues or profits. Future will also see a change in the financial and fiscal measure of a company to include more intangible items on the top-line besides margins and sales. The bottom-line of the firm cannot make contribution enough if it does not match the investor goals. Hence the investors and top leaders are two reps from firms, while the customers and distributors from the market side. The dealers are often ignored but play a very big role in taking the company to the leader slot. They can get the real details from the buyers and data on the market transitions. They are like the closest third-party for a company as they deal in the exteriors of a company and also interact with the buyers.

How Lean is Lean

They bring an unbiased view of the reach and gaps for the firms by involving in the lean. This is the line of lean that has to be followed by covering the key drivers in all chinks of the business. There is no scope for growth if the fissures in business are not seen and closed in time as the competitors would then take on those gaps. The market looks at the crevices of research, skill, man holes, machine lows, power and political gaps, leadership flaws and buyer focus with a scientific eye and tells the slow firms to work on the breaches or exit out of the sector or follow the leaders to gain up the pace. The markets can give lean firms a fairer chance than others. Those firms can promise better results than others as markets don't give free chance to any firm without taking a return either in the form of community projects or market growth. This growth can only help the

How Lean is Lean

firms in future tracking of new prospects and fat growth chance areas. The definite growth comes from lean because it gathers the best and throws out the worst of the business.

9 - The Lean Constituents - lean cycle, boosters, toners, next lean

The lean is the means to achieve the ends or market growth. For some testing reason, firms don't go lean but remain the way they are pulled or shaped by the market forces. But economy does not function on the forced characteristics.

Economies make their own paths and growth, hence companies that do so also progress in the front of economy so that they are noticed if the economy lags or the company. They grow with the economy and the economy reflects the strength of such industry and firms in its rates by putting the forerunners on the path to preferred business or trade for others in the world. They in turn become boosters of lean in the industries and

How Lean is Lean

unit firms. The wealth growth by lean is itself a different category of national development and sectors can create the toners of the economy. They can create fiscal or economic or political stability for the social progress or community welfare in the world. The nations grow if the entities grow because they accumulate wealth of various dimensions. It includes knowledge, skills, technologies, cross-border loyalties, royalties and quality. Any other seemingly beneficial factor to growth of an economy can also be included. The royalties include the profits and revenues or the growth in monetary terms. Again money is not the major factor and future is only going to prove this changing proclivity of money from wealth to welfare.

How Lean is Lean

The lean cycle starts with the initiation of the operations recording in terms of turnover, material consumed, power used, resources used etc. One particular operation can go through the different iterations and each has to be monitored separately. The inefficiencies have to be made into groups of weaknesses to be addressed in the shortest possible time and the lacunae fixed soon. The easiest way is to take the manuals and work strictly as per them. Or hire the best experts to take on those areas. Next is the pruning of wastage and unneeded parameters. All the extra resources can be routed into value-adding tasks. The JIT or Kanban activities can be adopted for more optimization and refinement in efficiency that can be increased to the last drop of the resource utilization. Hence the extra may be actually so because they are missing out on the intermediary steps so

How Lean is Lean

they have to be checked and worked up on. This is the step of rework or redesigns to make the processes best in output and least failing. The improvements may be mentored step-wise to achieve the best levels without jumping straight onto the top goal. It is easy to implement lean in ranges rather than reaching from one end to the other of the efficiencies. Measures can be used or the steps have to be ensured as per the new lean techniques. If a machine has to be worked on to make it reduce the defects then the steps of inducing right raw inputs, operating exactly as per function assigned, checking manuals, verifying output and taking remedial steps are needed for the phase-wise progress with the machine. Same is true for tools and technologies where programs and algorithms can be modified to fit the best outputs in the least time. The software and hardware

How Lean is Lean

can be tweaked with the help of experts to make them function best as per the company needs. The measures need not be always monetary but also method-wise. It is as necessary to follow the lean as getting the output. Lean is a fool-proof mechanism of getting at best business results without compromising on the other aspects of growth. It creates booster for the company at different steps through initiation, recording, pruning, rework, improve and modify. The boosters are like the rising grounds for business uplift to make the firm associated with markets instead of constant internal change. A firm has to adopt changes within more than often but when the market influencers are more in the reach and use of the firm, it gets better equipped to handle the change by being on the most informed side of the market. The boosters created by lean are the size, age, products,

How Lean is Lean

quality, time and price fronts. There could be others in the firm that may be related to the region, customer segment or technology version. The key boosters make sure that the company gains where others lose. Not all firms are able to win through markets though they are equally placed in the capabilities near full and opportunities near best.

They may use the tools to modify them to suit their needs and buyer demands, as in taking the support of past launches or ad-leveraging. The pieces of market gap-need-solution have to be fitted in well if the firms got to make it through the volatility and competition. Frequent changes or modification are needed to business to make it perform to the best expectation of the stakeholders. This is possible through toners or catalysts of business like relationship management

How Lean is Lean

(with customers, dealers, vendors), negotiation (with internal and external labor, partners et al), communication (events and policies on uniform foundation) and skills (knowledge, experience and core technical). These sound monotonous but occupy a big place on the corporate list. More than 80% business efforts fail here leading to loss-making deals or failed mergers or financial scandals or weak growth. The firms fail to notice or ignore them because they involve not a straight solution but layers of hierarchies or networks of business stakeholders. A business story takes a completely new turn if a segment of supporters takes a new stance. It gives a different result if a group of patrons take to a different approach from others. The next lean hence becomes juxtaposing to the exiting one. Each business can have thousands of routines and tasks thus

How Lean is Lean

making it a great basket of leans. We should get to work on each of them like a consultant prying on each business activity whether needed or not. A lot many times, when the business seemed to have settled on all accounts; the neat leans unsettle and create new challenges. The old leans change according to the new processes or initiative of the company and have to be revisited when they become non-lean or meaningless leans as described above. Lean is meaningful only if talks about efficiencies and performance. It need not talk about returns, goals, targets ranking on sales etc. This is important for those who are keen on making statistics a part of lean cycles. 80% efficiency speaks the entire story, 120% asks for probe too but to make out the best lessons and new scopes. For those firms that are consistently bothered about results, lean gives results on its

How Lean is Lean

end or may be even later if the spiralling effect of the business chain is to be believed. The cycle can vary as per the sectorial patterns and the firms need not bother much about it but the start since a good beginning is half the journey. After the initial lean, firms can get along the dots as lean is self-guiding. It creates the next in lean and firms can easily discover the ensuing and forward road on the keen front as lean opens up the to-do, as-is, without talking much on to-be until it is reached. The goal is on lean but is not bowling the managers on the start by beating them to jump at it. The lean is working to attain that goal and firm will do so in time and after lean is successfully applied. The real test of lean is in its use and not end. As lean does not end in a company's life, managers have to adopt it like linen on the robes of the daily business actions? Firms have to learn their methods of

How Lean is Lean

lean and what works for them won't always fit others. The lean in a firm is not solely resting upon the books but also on the corporate ends. The new firms try to copy lean from old or leaders but it is possible only in terms of the approach as to how much perseverance, dedication and time went into lean with a firm. The others have to lean on their staff orientation to fulfil lean. The manager can create or deviate a cycle, she can enhance the lean by boosting or hosting the cycle or even interrupt it by slow teams, they can initiate the toners to make the cycle work on the allied business factors like new flourishes, superfluities or treading milestones. They can lead to the new forms of lean or wire the old ones in continuum. Lean cannot be terminated as ineffective or unneeded step in the business and firms have to accept it before starting it. Or else lean can go

How Lean is Lean

unrecognized in business as ever since many firms do not want to waste time and resources on the reducing of market uncontrollable risk. Hence lean is not a annihilator of the market risk but manager of company operations and companies must not stop it once they start on it deliberately and as a different activity. Lean is a stimulant of the business to make it run along the lines of the paramount performance. There are many times that we adopt lean to understand the inefficiencies but it is only to say that the firms are opening their eyes and closing them most of the other times. Lean is the eye-opener and mentor of the business as it is known but it can reflect even without being treated so, when companies ignore the relevance and move onto another method, and later come back to lean but after it is late.

How Lean is Lean

The lean cycles can be boosters themselves because they create a systematic pattern for business growth with steps for next development and track of the old excellence. Lean demarcates process from the growth. The business may change and grow but the process remains same and that needs to be pulled up the levers of the volatilities. Firms may say that without goals they cannot work on lean. Deciding on the corporate objectives helps in meeting the ends through lean without losing focus of the goals because lean is itself a performance area. It is a method cum tool cum concept cum benchmark cum model. The model works with the sick units best to make them running, and the whole units to make them efficient. The benchmark measures the company progress along the lines of operational excellence. The concept guides the

How Lean is Lean

managers making them strict and educated about hula-boo creating tasks or teams. The method gives the ability to work on the business to derive the toners and boosters, removing the blocks and hurdles from the setups. The tool gets the nuances of the business fixed to work as per the stringent norms of the industry and market hiccups to resolve the delinking activities. Some of the business activities are rather isolated and can delink the existing business out of the area of precision. Such decisions are related the new equipment or expansions or radical products or new ways of working on the business activities. Such activities are adopted and deserted according to the results provided by them but the ones that don't need exclusion and should not be mediated are the lean measures or the business growth activities. No company can abandon the growth, so is

How Lean is Lean

lean too relevant and prioritised. The priorities cannot shift from lean once it is on because it directly links business to market outcome. A lean firm is followed for timeliness, exactitude, accuracy, yield, speed, decisioning and focus. The lean adjustments result out of the definite path of growth by competence and adeptness via need-based resource utilization and potential-based outcome retrieval. This is applicable to staffing as well as machine lean.

Every time the firms seem to be dependent on the same set of factors and working with the similar parameters of growth while conducting their business. It is true and still after centuries of industrial revolution we are not able to distil all the right factors at a given time because market presents volatilities at all times. A stable market is

How Lean is Lean

stagnant and cannot grow the economy or its functions. An economy functions on the services and industry along with the consumers. The economy does not grow any additional or new things other than the products and services. Its strengths are the skilled workers and favourable socio-economic-political environments. The industry functions on a sub-set of environment or the sub-environment related to a sector though all the factors are replicated on a minor level. The firms function on even refined environments that are prone to uncertainty and definite goal at the same time. Hence the job of companies to form good goals is itself tough. Saying a higher percentage or market number does not mean a good goal.

Often, firms fail because their goals are wrong. Firms become heavy or light

How Lean is Lean

depending on the internal solution – external need balance. Lean helps manage the rope on which the firm walks along with the pole of power that can hit on the wrong side if not held properly. Lean is always trying to balance the power and demands equation. A company cannot use the capabilities to meet small needs without adding some value. A firm cannot meet the market demands without adding some power to the governance mechanisms so that the future business activities are mentored well.

The length ranges from 3-12 months before yielding the first result. For those operations that are related to the parameters of time and end-to-end process the results take more than a year to show up. The ones with knowledge or skill-based parameters

How Lean is Lean

can turn out the efficiencies in the short-term.

The premium operations can be formed with repeat cycles or iterations of **learn-estimate-analyse-nurture** cycle. This works well when you are in the middle of a growth phase and want to gain out of the lean benefits. The firms can learn the lean areas needed to be improved, estimate the activity blocks or growth goals, analyse the change, pre/post-lean effect, and nurture the future lean. The learn step is a long one where the firms can do all research, examination and comparison to adopt lean either as new step or the next doable, from other units/departments/ rivals reaction or as market response. The managers can estimate the implementation cycle, resources and internal goals or methods. Here the necessary part is to

How Lean is Lean

understand the process and start on the lean. There is not a need to wait or delay in another study or time. The steps can be revisited as many times as needed and different team can be put on the internal or market study. The analysis of market feedback vs. internal procedures can open up a lot of scope for lean subdivision and application to parts of the business rather than all-at-once. The lean cannot function without the close-interaction of departments and tackling of dependencies. A plant that slows down the formation of company's products or goals can be leaned first followed by others to make the subsidiaries tied to the same company on standard or uniform practices. The variances must be able to notify the special changes required on firm or internal policies to bring about lean on a wider elevation. The level of lean to be adopted in the firm comes out on its own

How Lean is Lean

as the business grows and the efficiencies get affected. There is not a need for demarcation that the lean is heavy, medium or light as it is correlated to the business directly. More than the resources, the company must set aside the commitment and deliberation on lean. Again it must not be misconstrued as weekly meetings for 20 hours or a huge bulky tome of lean report. The stress must be and is on the lean cycles. The company must operate them if needed by sending the top managers from their AC cabins into the remote production areas or the supply-chain functionaries to obey the rules of the lean. They may be failing at places rather ignored by all for convenience or fear. Lean enables the differences to be overcome by converting convenience into motivation and fear into opportunity. The simple cycle of a lentil-cleaning unit might bring out scope for change in its

How Lean is Lean

sieve-wash-dry process to wash-dry-sieve to make it more efficient. The slight shift may being out the motivation to come early to office to finish the first half before evening so that the solar energy can be used to save on the resource utilization. The fear of labor unrest may incite the chance for better deals on overtime as the workers are better rested and they also get a chance to find the faults of the suppliers providing as with more waste or less waste, along with avoiding the wastage if washed upfront. The workers get a better inspection chance for the material before and after processing to make out the cause if proportion of waste in impurities-good matter is high if washed before sieving than later thus letting the unused to go waste rather than the pure matter.

How Lean is Lean

The employees must be aware and involved in lean in many ways possible whether as implementers, supervisors, assessors, auditors, analysts or delegators. There are external parties but the internal teams must be working on them in at least the minimum required lot. They should not leave the discovery and application to separate teams to get exclusive learning. The boosters, toners and next leans can be understood well if the same team is involved in the different steps by deploying different resources on the task without dividing the team on each task. A team can discuss at two levels – internally to collate the findings and externally to aggregate the contribution. The teams may vary in the degree of the involvement based on their department's fault in the overall deficiency. The teams can share the interdepartmental tasks to make the

How Lean is Lean

third-party lean possible within the firm. Hence the constituents of lean are dependent on the type of the process improvements that the firm is looking at.

The lean is going to make the firm effective, industry more competitive and economy stronger.

10- Projects and non-Customer Projects

The lean can be differentiated based on projects that related to customers and not. The firms all work for their internal growth and external share in the market. The need for internal growth may be out of customer instigated feedback or not. The external is mostly for the customers and rarely otherwise as the face of the brand is the customer. The differentiation is to broaden the lean on the specific operations related directly to buyers and those due to the stakeholder interests. Companies have to change their internal policies to gain the competence among employees or to gather momentum in the organizational best practices. A firm can create the best methods by constantly innovating and excelling beyond its targets. The firms can add value to market practices by adopting lean on the core or

How Lean is Lean

customer related processes. A company that leans out the call-centre without working on the internal employee conduct can put the brand at a risky line from where a single employee default can throw the company into stagnations.

There are many projects and tasks that involve no customer orientation and are aimed at gaining the capabilities within. The firm can redirect such tasks to the lean for making primary and secondary studies exactly pertinent to the market need. This matching between customer and non customer projects can create a perfect lean in the company without risk for future. If companies blindly cut down on their resources to make lean business operate out of different locations to a single one even, then they face the risk of market volatility or customer unacceptability. The buyers

How Lean is Lean

wont accept such firms in the long-run. As at the end of the lean cycle, the customers must accept the improvements as worthy of paying for in the form of their energized products or services. The new or improved output must add appeal to the customers and value must flow down from the inert company to the active customers. A company may be prone to inertia but its customers are active in analysing competitors before taking a favourable or un- decision for the firm's product purchases. The flow of lean from internal to external in the form of the effects is important for customer to change perceptions about the brand or products.

The flow of lean from external to internal happens when forced by the market, so it is better that the firm adopts lean

How Lean is Lean

before being forced by the market. Such lean is also propping from the economy that moulds the market to act in favour of GDP growth and lifestyle trudge. The GDP does not grow if the yield does not improve and garnish the citizens' life. A rising GDP without adding the vim in the people's – students, employees, housewives, seniors, special – lifestyle is a valueless regime.

The education can be improved without adding to GDP but the reverse is not favourable to economy. If an economy cannot sustain literacy then it cannot sustain the growth. If the workers are not free to move between jobs then their career growth is hampered, thereby slowing the productivity. The responsibility of industry does not end there but percolates to the life of homemakers who want to prepare their

How Lean is Lean

families to a successful contribution in the economy. They should get new options to grow whether through the savings schemes or the consumer purchases offers. The inflation becomes more important for control to energize the home folks. The range of industry growth thus encompasses different segments of the society without marking any return from them. There are many segments of consumers that cannot contribute to the economy like infants, old, disabled or convicted. They should be led to proper channels of growth or grooming. The two sectors of population - old and special needs cannot be expected to contribute much except on their will and wish by advisory or cheering up. It is the onus of the companies to add value even for them. Lean is hence important to know where to expect return and not. If the lean is worked on a non-customer project the

How Lean is Lean

return is the indirect distant sampling that comes from the improved entity operations or design. Imported products are not always cheap because they involve the customer preference more than the cost of shipping. The lean comes of import of the value that has to be persisted in all the products of that nation.

When working on lean, it may thus seem to be totally patriotic and internal but the effects can come from and go to outside too thus making it cross-country development.

The customer projects may become non if the lean does not translate into their products. A lean change to make the task 110% efficient can reduce the response time for the client-vendor tasks but the same is not useful to the

How Lean is Lean

customer at the end of the value chain. The aim of the lean when it started may be to bring down change in the pricing but the price is not that important for the purchase decision for the given product or the price could not be reduced due to some other creepages in lean. Either ways, the customer is not the beneficiary of lean so she cannot be expected to appreciate the lean unless she gets to know or understand the importance in long-term. Companies in Japan don't have loyalties based on direct customer benefits but on the level of the corporate excellence. The bullet trains have not become strength because commuters see the benefits from day 1 but they had invested in the new technologies by buying into the fast-track rails. Now they and we see the benefits from continued operations as a few millions bucks per (each) mile of track cannot be justified by any

How Lean is Lean

advantages. The lean thus is not from the cost or ostentation but the real dedication to the welfare on a lean scale for the large community. The lean scale welfare is possible by converging the best resources and frequent buyers to give a need and a solution meeting the need. This is not so easy and needs a lot of grilling of markets and capabilities, devoting the technologies to innovation and rising corporate excellence. The operational excellence that starts with non-customer projects may sometimes go to customer advantage. But a company should never start with lean with the idea of gaining customers. The goal of lean is the progression but not a measure. The path of lean is the development and advance but not a destination. The lean projects are hence all related to the company's growth and customer delight. The next step is customer loyalty and the

How Lean is Lean

recommendation or referencing. The last step is the direct goal of all companies today but it does not reach the last step by targeting the networking or referrals. The reward systems and offers can work if the customers are shown real packages of loyalty. The credit cards provide free trips or fuel refills as loyalty rewards. But the durables firms provide the same at gaped costs that ask the availors to pay for the discounted products or as an added purchase. The incentive would be add the prix from the company side to give a stay or free coupon for next time to the beneficiary. The customers behave like the freely served and the firms become benefactors finicky about the rising costs of free gifts. But the corporate mind-sets have to change when they expect every pie of their salary to be paid by work or to recover the offers in other products or to charge

How Lean is Lean

annual fee to make customers share their costs of loyalty programs. Sharing corporate expenses come to be part of many lean programs but this is harmful to the long-term prospects and interests of the company. Often, the competitors copy the same model as if to prove it right by making it repeat.

Two rights can sometimes make a wrong. The expenses of credit-rationing, background surveys etc. have to be borne by the companies. It is for their safeguarding of the limits and credit risk but not for the benefit of the card users.

The users opposed the entire use of the ATM when a fee was levied by banks in a series as if to make it right. It had to be taken off because the people were well back to hectic bank activity thus blocking the traffics in banks for withdrawals. Hence certain innovations

How Lean is Lean

need to be pushed at the company cost. The same users, we, don't mind paying extra for a home-delivery shopping because it is more out of our need and not the store's need to vacate the spot. That activity eases our time for going out with family or working on household chores. Thus lean must be applied to make things easier for customers without necessarily making them costlier than ever.

Lean has to be more than applied on the online lifestyles that are becoming inflated day by day. The costs seem to be controlled but they are neither for the buyer nor for the companies. The Companies estimate a 9% higher spend on internet business than otherwise. The reasons are because the traditional business had its entire value chain

How Lean is Lean

formed and functioning; the new mode is still to consolidate on the chain.

The lean is helpful here. The buyers anyway tend to pay more to the internet seller as each transaction though compared on the best prices gets bloated on the extra handling charges or shipping costs or other inflated fee.

The start and end of lean depends on the transition. A large lean project can be divided into the small lean projects and activities can be tracked and measured but the measure of lean by customer or revenue per se is not appropriate. The lean transformation takes years for affecting the markets and even the internal operations. Each change has to be managed to avoid side-effects on the other corporate functions or projects.

How Lean is Lean

The monitoring lasts for as long as the lean and lean lasts for as long as the market. This is a shortcut economic view to development as the other route could be to work on interest rates, deficits, inflation and currency. The lean enables economy to be lean without negating the industry growth. It is all-inclusive advance of the economy. The economy can also grow without adding value to the industry as is happening for the past few years globally on account of slowdowns or sudden interest spurts or other fallouts. The reasons can be politically rooted but they are ever-present in the world. Therefore the fragile firms have to balance the high-level market changes with the low-level customer demands with the nano-level corporate variations that are induced or generated by internal or external environments.

How Lean is Lean

The markets act like scavengers on the firms when they pick on each loophole and push the firm down the gutter of failure or test. Weak firms take no time in revealing their gaps for others to win through the competition. Strong firms take time to understand other's reaction in the market, other's perceptions and interpretations before launching a response or cover their internal weaknesses before coming in the market with a new proposal or strategy. Such a strong growth propels the ecosystem in the progressive direction and drives the nation in the positive angles. A nation is not growing like a bamboo but as a tree with branches, fruits near different angles of the trunk. The straight-line growth vs. angular growth makes lean vary as per the required line of operation and prevalent gaps in the existing business model.

How Lean is Lean

Generally, customer projects are not possible without lean in angular directions because they ask for low price today, better technology tomorrow, easy pay next month and variants or colours later. These may switch in the middle of a lean cycle and the need for another lean comes in with the multiple leans working on the business at the same time.

Lean can sometimes provide space to the companies to act in accordance with their preference. Markets have seen the times not quite too often but often that firms have topped the business ranks by working on the corporate decisions rather than the market demands. Microsoft is one example that everyone knows of. It often happens in pricing but the area of products or innovation can also run by the drift. Johnson (JNJ) had

How Lean is Lean

put forth many products when market did not need but the diagnostics evolved on their equipment after their innovation.

Simple products are made new or so complex or stylish or innovative mostly against the buyer demand because they don't envisage the trimmings or trappings. The lean has to be fitted into the pieces of the firm's preferences and buyer's to get the most cost-effective solution for the market. Though lean does not need cost reduction for the firm it needs the same to be passed on to the buyer. The inherent complexity of conceding the benefits not earned for the firm but distribution to the customers is the lean weight. The projects get the weight of lean and nothing else thus making them the lean executors if the lean experts are not hit on the pay. They go where the pay seems more but the

How Lean is Lean

firms can go anywhere to use lean as an operations pacifier in the business. It removes the unnecessary steps and includes the ones leading to growth. The finesse of lean does not get eroded or corroded with repeated application but it only gets enhanced by use of the method to simplify the corporate practices. The tools that cannot make the business grow become the growth gears and small gaps are covered without even being aware of them. The lines of business that seem to be held with the lagging metrics and slogging routes get the new scopes and changes for the alliance of the market and firm interests. Lean is the connector between the new demands and old successes. When companies become lean, even the new scope arises as per their path of growth and capabilities. The firms know how to tackle market errors and earn the mileage on the customer

How Lean is Lean

loyalty by making them part of the future corporate events. A company invites top customers for dinners or parties to part their thoughts on the growth paths and patterns of lean management. Often this is the pin area for the company to focus its lean on as the users of a company know better than the sellers. The customers are the users of a firm rather than its products. They buy into the smallest decision of the firm when they pay for their products.

The sales are not the drivers of the lean but lean is a driver of sales. A fit company is used by the buyer for being a part of her home or family life. The more a firm is used the more it works towards lean and the more lean a firm works for the better it is able to make itself fit. It is suitable for the market and for the consumers. A lean need not be

How Lean is Lean

made into project but project can be made lean by simple tweaking of performance factors like deadlines, budgets, scope, resources, process etc. This is again a narrow example of lean and the broadest lean is the organizational culture that allows for sincere employees to work on any stream as per their skills and needs. They are also rewarded as human beings all need to be motivated by carrot and stick at different times in their career. Machines can be efficient to the core but not men.

The firms that lean on non-lean measures finally get stuck with the wrong opportunities or decisions or wastage of resources with over-utilization. Lean is not applicable if the firm reverses the curtailed activities in the name of stopping lean or adopting some other method. The management tactics are all aligned in such a way that no one method interferes with others. Often companies give the condition of fitting with another method to get the results from a given method. Lean does not stop Kaizen nor the other way round. Some methods are internal and some are external but on the whole, the tools and tactics are meant for the organizational growth and development. The methods do not obstruct or de-facilitate other methods as all of them are aimed towards the health of business and the firm's overall progress.

11- Milestones in Lean

The companies do not monitor the lean goals but the milestones are railed to find out the progress of lean. The goals

How Lean is Lean

are not relevant to the extent of monetary pinning as detailed earlier. The firms deem essential the lean in form and shape of the business. That is more pertinent than getting a % hike here and there. The various points in the journey are the start, progress and transition. Transition is any turn or re-visiting by restarting the lean on a different scale or dimension. The companies work on starting the lens of lean and the key milestones are the development of the firm on related parameters like initial changes in the team efficiencies, business reposes, firm differentiation and narrow or broad scope. The progress works on the next levels like testing success, team growth, project efficiency and product success.

The transition phase includes the final parameters like product excellence,

How Lean is Lean

customer allegiance, vendor efficiency and other value-adds. The milestones are all important for the business to know where it stands and where it needs to go by using lean. As firms anyway use the lean, do they have to track it? Yes because they need to spread the work across the firm to make others accept lean and spread the word to enable them to nourish the confidence in lean. No when the companies get bogged down by the numbers or targets so tightly that they are really on a demotivating path for employees. Managers want to blame the subordinates and chuck them out instead of the correction measures that have to be adopted across the width and height of the firm. The company wide measures should be understood only to implement them and not raise money against them. Not constricting the path of lean with such material or

How Lean is Lean

tangible ties will make lean work for the entire body of organization. All the related entities would also benefit by lean in such cases. The firm would see a better overall benefit taking shape in all its businesses. Hence the free lean would be a maximiser of the whole firm. But firms need to get to the goads of lean in how it is forcing a change or pushing a progress or thrusting a development within the company. The companies related to the sector would then see synergies along with the gaps for competing. The firms in unrelated sectors would see the generality and specificity of their business lean. The lean sounds like a major asset for the firms because if they are able to be so then they can walk out of the narrow shell of corporate shackles and fly in the broad skies of new expanse or scope. The changes for big business are related to the data intelligence that also

How Lean is Lean

comes with lean. The big data can grow the firm in very broad levels and top levels, after which lean brings the small data from within the realms of the business by chipping in along with the other parties of vendors, buyers, dealers, facilitators, agencies et al. The level of high or low progress does not come from data that can add only some insight to the business. The firms cannot fight for data but can sight on data. Lean creates the big and small data by working on the exteriors and internal environment of the companies. The various departments can take lean data to analyse their past and future trends against the current developments. The existing sequential progress is possible through lean and the companies can gain new insights into the operational and customer patterns. The internal growth comes from big data and the external growth comes from small data.

How Lean is Lean

The customers give the small data and the tools give big research data for new facets to be led to new decisions about the business next. The entities manage data by analysing or remodelling but the real use of data is in predicting and past analysis. Past data is dealing with reality. Present data is prone to change. Future data is totally unreal. The data cannot hold any weight but we give it as the future is uncertain. The users or buyers can hold no obligation to tally the data to facts but go in any direction with their decisions about the purchases or investment in the firms. The guts of firms lie not on the data crunching but on the user analysis. The most useful part of lean comes in analysis of users when the talk moves to data. Users of end-, patrons, process-, or intermediary levels are all able to throw some light on the real market needs. They can give

How Lean is Lean

data on the small changes that can give big progress to the companies. Big changes can give small steps to the firms but small ones can make the firms go from one step of market to the higher level of headship.

Managers should align the different goals to the lean initiation so that the correct points of check arise while in the business. It's not a separate or distinct thing to do lean but it is a business as usual to follow lean. So as not to abhor the managers with unrealistic numbers or goals, the lean must be fixed on milestones and daily benchmarks. The daily benchmarks are the ones that should not be deviated at all not even for once, like the machines and tools or the packages that must be on, off or maintained at the given slots of time as the deviations can alter their

How Lean is Lean

performance and create obstacles in the other departments. The lean miles are full of to-the-point (TOP) business. The TOP is the means to get done the business activities that would otherwise hover over the stretches that cause delay and wastage in execution, resources or time. TOP is the direct attack on the weaknesses and justifying the lean to fulfil the optimum requirements. The needs are not all relevant though may come from the users or markets flat. Some needs ought to be managed well before the launch of their product forms. They have to be studied and innovated to make them lifestyle friendly. The old fairy tales characters are today's smurfs. If they ask for a new Snowhite she has to come from today's corners and cant be left to die by eating an apple. The apple business will then be in fix. They need to be studied in terms of how their needs fit

How Lean is Lean

with the others or along the markets. A smurf who asks for a flying saucer cannot be sold just as he needs it or his coterie wants it. We need to build the resources and needs to find the lean fit between the markets and companies. Markets try to make the companies compete on the rough road and toughest sides of business. Companies are on their marks to find the fastest route to growth to race past others. Customers find their companies to be the need-resolver who build the resources for the end-user. A firm possesses a limited range of resources that it reengineers and forms a different type of resource for the other processors to work upon, who work on them to convert in to a more useable resource group. The final resource pool available to the buyer is the product pool or service silo that goes to them and their families to alter their life. Lean

How Lean is Lean

enters each tune to make it suitable to the given set of participants. Thus it adds value when it makes the managers ignore the good features and work towards better ones. It enhances utility when the seller demos the products without expecting the buyer to invest her money into it. They make her buy by telling the good points, rewarding her with freebies, adding loyalty points to her lifestyle and giving references to new products of higher versions or newer models of future. The innovation behind lean is to make lean new each time the firm uses it. Lean has no given shape or image, so the firms are free to lend their shades and weights attributing their values to the lean so that the end-buyer can know where the lean is making her products lean too thus adding worth to her lifestyle by removing wastage and defect rates.

How Lean is Lean

The import of the lean and the role of the business in lean are not too different. Lean needs business as the strong powerful concept is of no use when not used by the firms. Today we don't see any mandate upon lean but firms hold it as they need any help in walking through the market of volatilities. But the day the firms start talking to lean and holding it every day in one or the other unit of theirs, the lean would gain better response and results too coz the more the lean is used the more it will be able to help business and the firms need not feel guilty of using lean when desired. The lean gives more beneficial results if it is used as a regular business application like Outlook or lunch. Incorporate lean into the tasks and life of the entity and employees. Let them interpret what they want for the word is too focused to be go reverse or brash or wary. Let the units use lean

How Lean is Lean

and show them to the managers – just how they are using – instead of – where they are getting the results – it's good for later status if they get to this also. Let them come and share the experiences instead of results. Slow down the chasing of targets because if running could give gains, then all companies would do the same. Let the insights, ideas and dedication gain business importance rather than the profits or customers. Adding 3 clients per week makes no great business as that means that either the business is too favourable or the market timing is too good. Such times are not the ones to last forever or for long. Lean times also don't last forever and hence the milestones should be used as meaningful deviants when the lean ends. Working on a new business line gives the growth but it also gives the ability to fight with the non-lean obstacles while tending on the

How Lean is Lean

useful tactics in business. It's like shifting the attention from a non-lean to a different lean. We are not escaping or evading it but trying to solve by adding value on another note. The firms that compete for the good of customers often do so because they want to divert their eyes from a direct issue to a related solution. Deviating fix from the issue gives the time to find its solution, focusing on creation of other strength, gives the confidence to tackle the issue.

$$(1 + x)^n = 1 + \frac{nx}{1!} + \frac{n(n-1)x^2}{2!} + \dots$$

The binomial theorem is too easy as it involves only probabilities and yes-no scenarios or success-failure potions but it can help bodies predict the traffic or the data analysis in detail. It is compact

How Lean is Lean

and powerful by its mention of confidence, sampling and expectations. The more complex forms give the ranges and options of working on the capacities or ratios. It can give trends or combinations for the building of the scenarios or to be more exact, the mining operations in a firm. Lean can be made to work on such new ideas by using the regular life maths to make efficiency business. This is the real Math and not the ones taking revenues or margins or few mechanical ratios. They are the related set of calculations for the subject but the innovation that is inherent in Maths has to be suggested by the Consultants working in firms. After all, we don't learn to take exams but to work with it. Lean also is not a book thing but work thing. It is a working thing and can make broken firms work. The managers can look at it with a student lens as lean can get new things

How Lean is Lean

in each cycle. Work on it to make more on it. Selling is the last step of business and firms today want it to be on right from day 1, it's good for talks not for walks. Still given the technological we must take a diabolical approach to make the employees fight for goals from day 1. Goals are their rights in the current business world and they have a right to prove them on the goals. So does the firm have a right to thrust the duty to run after goals? The workers and top employees must be given definite hard goals to run after as the education makes them able to do so. If they don't do then they must be mentored or fired. The reason why firms start with the end today is that the resources are equipped with skills and knowledge of that high calibre. Often, the employee claims a much higher reward and companies need to and end up paying more than 10x the worth of the work delivered by

How Lean is Lean

her due to the merit of the degree or college and this myth stays for more than decades till the lean comes in. It makes the top leaders realise that their pay has to be less than their effort if they have to keep the open route to learning and excellence of ideas. Companies have to take a stand and make low their pays by at least 50% even if threatened by employees for resignation. Make it a point of facing the employees and offer them low pay because they ask for more than 10 times what they are worth based on the inflated egos or the bloated targets. The value is much less than showcased when it reaches the end user. Banks often become a prey to the hygiene factors when the top Directors and VPs deliver nothing by taking everything of the company and its laborious lot. The workers are different from the makers. The top half makes the pay and perks

How Lean is Lean

by delegating or merely playing critics and being advisors. But the reality is that whoever works for a company is serving God (customers), and hence needs to 'work' whether CEO or clerk. Work is the single word with a single meaning and cannot change forms according to titles or designations. The VP cannot say that her work is only to give the credit of her college or presence by her graceful room board or the few looks or talks to make other feel her presence or authority. She has to take pen and screen to work on the numbers that she boasts of being certified or dealing in her past successes. Just as earning does not stop, the work should also not stop on the pretext of already done in the past or the level being that of supervisor. Anybody can talk as the mouth is free. Anybody cannot learn and work on the ultra-tough concepts or Maths of the

How Lean is Lean

business and so the capable ones *must* work but not remain happily settled that they are the esteemed ones to possess the degrees. If they don't do who else would or can? The national economics face mismatch because the blue-collared workers do not try to participate but remain lavish mute spectators whose words only cost a bomb. The employees must all talk and discuss with those on all other hierarchies to make them understand the business dynamics and learn their hurdles. Sharing knowledge only increases it and still does not diminish it even if we are in the most modern of the technological naïve times. We can find fault in business but it is not easy to work on a solution or process to rectify it. Lean can help us in knowing our worth and role in the company. If I know about how to bring down the defect rate then I must do it in a day or week but not leave to

How Lean is Lean

my inexperienced or low-qualified staff to wrestle for 6 months to do the same thing. Then they should be paid higher than an MBA because they do it without an MBA. The degree of sturdiness in business approach and marks or certificates in student state is vastly different. The same degree cannot be applied to work and joining. It is useful to prove the ability to guide others and not to earn more money. A non-degree manager can earn more by using her experience at work rather than a one using her aura in work. Aura is needed but along with the hard-core hardworking skills instead of harrowing delegations or deadlines for pay hikes or bonuses. Often managers claim that they grew the business from 10 to 50% or the margins from so n so. The single-handed credit is not so as the team has worked on it in selling, dealers, grilling buyers, meeting clients, building

How Lean is Lean

products etc. The idea also doesn't come from her. She only gets the title of being efficient enough to take the team success credit and she would not shy away from taking responsibility of failure as her stakes are not at loss in any way otherwise she wouldn't take the blame. Sometimes, the appraisals or bonus schemes seem to be fake or only meant for the top risers who can influence the bosses in any direction.

The aim of lean is to make the business excellent and so the employee treatment as uniform and not swayed by black mail or white mail. The employees must also be shown stick long to make them appreciate the worth of carrots fed to them earlier, without creating an imbalance in the firm's performance. When a good employee leaves, she is offered a chance to re-join or a pay hike

How Lean is Lean

to rethink, but when a poor employee leaves, he is not made to rethink, it simply means that the firm is weak as it could not groom the worker to raise in the work levels. The aim of lean is also to unveil such lacunae and set the company rolling on its agile track of making weak into strong employees. They should also be made to be included in the group, not because they cant pay a fee but because they got the equal brinks to raise up if given a finger of direction or show or hike. Firms may laugh if they are told to offer a hike to a worst leaving employee but some firms do it. A firm in oil sector gave a promotion and hike to make their average manager stay in along with the option of working from home. She grew up to the level of expanding the firm in six other locations using that perk. She is selling oil to companies who are selling it in their brands along with

How Lean is Lean

creation of local brands for the firm also. Another poor employee got a hike and she stayed back too making the company grow by a quarter as such perks don't go unrecognised by the employees. Also, the firm must balance between the internal goals of employees vs. projects. Both should be taken into account while working on the growth. It is true that workers grow with company but only hours of arrival-departure in office or extra-curricular or client feedback or gender or bosses' feedback is not enough to make or break the career. Competition is not on third-grade parameters but on merit and knowledge. The risk-taking appetite of employees is often considered as the danger posed by the worker or the expense route of the intelligence but firms that detail those initiatives can halt up into the leaders rung. The patterns of employees differ and all want to make a difference

How Lean is Lean

to the company that is not recognized for different political or apolitical reasons known to us. Education or degree or lack of it does not make the morale of employees to take the company to higher flat. The growth of companies need to be boosted in all possible ways and that is what lean teaches us. Intelligence costs us a stone not only as it is rare diamond in some minds, it is also used by some only. The business intelligence is also like that and weighs heavy though used and owned by few. It needs not only degrees but also experience to juggle with varied business developments in the market. The market does not allow for the good companies to become better unless they prove it by their skills, employees and customers. All have to talk in favour of company but for an employee her work should be enough to talk for her as the others may choose to be reticent. It is

How Lean is Lean

not their mistake but their privilege to remain so. The elegant employee is not expected to fight for the voice to support her but waits to get it due or use skills to move to another firm. As no firm recalls a group of people but projects and skills better than names, the exiting people are hardly material to the company or the new hires. The lean created by them goes a long way and the firm grows beyond times as it is the dedication of few employees who don't leave the trail without a major recognition that makes the firms market leaders too. Lean is a task, it is not a label. It cannot buy you the brands and customers but it can fit them into your business so that you can sell it to them on better terms. The firms improve their activities to get aligned on the track of expectations and conditions of market demands and user requests. The firm cannot becomes unconditional or without any expectations just as the

How Lean is Lean

employees or clients or the other value-adders to the business. The firms don't get lean by leaving their profits or clients but they don't either by pestering them to no end. Often companies get profits when they leave them to the success stones of better performances and deliverables. If such firms don't get profits, then also they remain agile and lean to be flexible enough to adapt to any market demand in any time. There are companies that get success by running after it in the name of focus or goal, but they face inflexible or non-lean structures that cannot adapt to business changes. The main objective is to make the company worth setting goals and most of us do that without getting our business fully functional. The race is on forever but we must take some time off in enabling our business drivers to help us become lean and strong in the market. Such firms can attain success for long-term to make their business relations sustainable and galvanising for the others to participate in its growth.

12 - Timing the Lean

Which firms do not want to get the timing right on markets, clients and employees? Lean is ignored on the fact that it is too internal or part of business but timing is needed for lean. When a company is going down in all its operations then lean helps them to pep up the figures. Such lean may not fit the term but it is lean also. Managers must adopt lean when the market is not a fighter. The market should be in the normal state so that the lean is starting on a normal phase. Of lean when it starts in a crisis the lean tends to stop after the crisis or it is seen as a rescuer.

How Lean is Lean

Lean as said is the same business tactic that keeps it running every day and lets it cope with crunch without much gain of rust.

The time of lean when it strays from the non-lean is also worth noting as the non-elements can change and have to be recorded within a short variation. A major change is not out of lean as lean works in lean movements. The time of lean changes are long for small ones and accumulate for time. A stretch of lean does not stretch the change or time but the lean has to be followed with a new fire to get the lean props in tie of the goals of firm. Each goal can be treated as a lean benchmark if it is to do with long-term use and sustenance of business. A new profit though 50% more than earlier cannot make the lean good for the firm after 14 years but a new

How Lean is Lean

dynamic or zeal can do so even for 140 years.

Lean is good as long as the company is working on it. Once the firm gets complacent and relaxes with past lean results, non-lean forms up into inertia and poor business. The growth factors are all held back by the firm as its resources divert into non-growth areas and unproductive activities. The arid lands develop for company making it unfertile and non-renewable success. Usually firms adopt lean because it builds up success by making the corporate charter strong. The firms also try to attain success in such a way that they get the next success by the same track in a minor different way. The market changes can be thus easy for the firms and the success can be

How Lean is Lean

repeated. If non-lean is formed then the success areas get parched by unneeded risks and volatilities. The frequent key of success is the lean as it gives the confidence and agility needed for business ties. The ties of firm with market and economy get the growth synergistic. As the firm gets alienated from economy the growth becomes sporadic and gradually the success leaves the firm to envelop it in the night of failure. Lean firms can overcome the failing times by learning from or by so neatly averting the weeds that the firms get to work on new goals that are easy or scope friendly. When big firms complain that the size is stopping them from moving ahead that is wrong, the weight stops them from moving on but not the size. The weight stops them because the burden of market scoping, research drill down or slowdown, customer guilt arising from the gaps in

How Lean is Lean

needs vs. tasks or poor quality or misperceptions, employee balancing with the personal vs. career vs. corporate goals all lead to lean but by force. Such lean helps in curing rather than preparing the firm for the business excellence. Lean as a medicine is not long-term or regular in use, need or impact. The managers have to reinitiate such lean so that it is taken in the right stride by the employees, stakeholders and customers. The customer guilt is the burden of displeasing clients by false hypes or ignoring their real needs for wrong reasons or the sale on wrong gestures of price, parity or value. The good firms avoid the customer guilt from clouding the internal policies as not to miss out on the speed of the decisions or implementations of strategies. They either sort it out with citing the real statistics with clients or work on presenting the right solutions or leave it

How Lean is Lean

to clients for further guidance on their needs or demands to provide a product to suit their lifestyles.

The gaps in lean and non-lean are mainly related to timing. A wrong timing can make a lean attribute into lot. Lean into lot stands no work or effort but timing. If a product is got on timing that is not fit with the clients' needs, it raises costs or wastage due to non-purchase or deviant innovation. If a machine is operated on wrong slots then defects come into products. It is as simple. The lean also gets into flaws or errors states if it is not adopted at right times as one after the other, all steps miss out on the timing making the work ineffective or gapped. The firms fight to get lean right when they interact with rivals' customers, or respond to rivals, react to the competitors rather than mince the

How Lean is Lean

differences, toggle up or down in the market but not accept the lean. Such resistance also creates a gap in lean timing. Firms must muster the courage to take lean steps when needed. A talk or tactic after lean is capable of adding a lot more vigour to the entity than without lean. The lean after or before the timing is not totally poisonous or detrimental but it delays the results, that was due on time. If companies miss out on the timing success also deviated from timing. If firms get the right mix of lean and time, the market also gets the right mix of success and growth for the firms on time. Lean has to be timed perfectly for getting it into the realms of business growth for a consistent period of time and with sustainable value to all the involved parties of business. The firms that get to work with the different parties of ecosystem in the business are luckier than those making it alone to the top.

How Lean is Lean

The market ladder let all grow equally but those in the ecosystem get to make the most out of lean by adding value to the remote stakeholders who then rely on the firm without an iota of doubt. Thus it gives the permanent success and not one on. To get away from lean is to get away from the business line. The firms enter into the line of business with the intention of being in business in *the* business way.

Lean is the way of the business. It gets timed on its own if practised as a regular business way rather than as a mechanism to earn smelting profits out of it. If made a way, lean can become the business excellence tool and profit-making mechanism on its own. But business should be left to lean. The competitors must be left to copy or imitate or follow the lean companies as

How Lean is Lean

then also the rivals would bring in new scope only for the firm in lead and lean. If they don't dare copy then they leave the entire ground to the lean business. Flourish or nourish, let lean do it the business way. It's hard to trust a word and leave the entire business dreams to it but it works. Lean works to make others tough to cultivate the entire business into a successful and innovative one. The companies in different sector feel like moving between industries or expanding because they cannot work with lean. It is not that easy to work with lean. Lean is not lean to work with but we should adopt lean. The firms that worked on lean earned more chances to work on lean in future thus earning lean with lean. The timed lean earns more time for lean in future. Thus the lean gives lean for the future so that the returns on lean become more real and felt by business. The barons don't

How Lean is Lean

exist to make the business heavy by weight but by lean. A heavy lean is one firm whose market responses are all timed however small and cannot be ignored by competitors, markets, customers and stakeholders. Barring the few moments of stress when any business cant kneel on market timing, firms must bend themselves to work on lean timing. Their heads have onward looking path on lean unlike the eyes that never look down on the path. It is better to be a student of lean than a master of non-lean business. Even companies like GE couldn't have excelled if they had not adopted lean in the right time, whether often or once in a while. The leaders don't have to crib about anything if they have lean on their minds. Businesses that work on the hectic path of circuitous fretting on customers and employees to achieve a lot in a short time lose out on lean and

How Lean is Lean

then on everything else as it can taper off the success line. The timing on lean is not that tough or complex to decide. It needs alacrity and event analysis by the companies once in a month at least. If a single analyst can dedicate herself to the task on a daily basis then that also creates the time sense among the corporate leaders to adopt lean as a trick of business. The trick only tricks other failures to put the company on the path of customers and success. Being with customers does not always mean profits or sales or brand. It means being in business with others and not isolated or alone.

The typical businesses work on simple model of hire-produce-sell. This is the model that works and has been working for decades. The need of the times is to time each step to suit the business. The

How Lean is Lean

hiring of right people with right skills on right time is going to help get the management of the firm running on smooth tracks. The task of producing or creating service or product or resource for further processing or next step should be done with efficiency, market shrewdness, outsourcing sense, value-add and timing to make sense to the market. If all televisions would have been produced now instead of decades ago, imagine the plight of markets and customers in dealing with the wrong timing of products. Make them when they are needed then you won't regret even if they don't sell. The last step of sell is after ensuring that the product is ready to do so. The cycles may repeat or forms may change or displays may handle differing packaging needs, but the sale has to happen to the end-user or processor or dealer to manage the entire payment processing and

How Lean is Lean

distribution of the service or product. In all this, comes technology as a crucial enhancer and it adds value to the entire stream of business by creating or destroying the delinkers or uplinks demanded by the business. The times are changing and firms must too. Firms that reply too much to the clients or vendors waste time on branding rottenly as all stakeholders know what to expect and throw open areas for controversy or argument only to raise the bars for others. It is easy to find faults and throw gauntlets at others instead of facing up to one on own. The firms don't like simple value chains and like to make them complex by saying that they cannot work on the 3-step business. Some of them call hire-make-borrow-buy-fire-outsource-test-pack-distribute-sell-return-reward. It is not tough to say that it's the same model with the different colours added so that the path

How Lean is Lean

looks tougher to appreciate. Simple business models are also appreciated and in fact they run into champions or winners as they don't embellish their operations with heavy processes but remain lean. The firms manage just to scrape through yearly targets without staying or doing much to stay in the business of business.

Some quotes - The lean is the backbone of the economy and its constituents for only the best can be lean and lean can be best if the environments changes are balanced well.

The non-lean is not lost into the failures always but it has more risk than lean.

Business stands on volatility and virtual pillars of market, customers, employees and economy, any of which can falter at

How Lean is Lean

any time leaving the non-lean or lean into shatters.

Market admires the lean business as that gives more space to others and sustains on the maker or market superiority without the fear as churned by non-lean firms that are big in size and seem to be capable of thrashing the markets in a single mistake or strategy.

How Lean is Lean

13- Lean times vs. Now or Then

The lean times are always and are modern in every time. In the olden days, lean educated men through experience. Today men are certified in lean first and then experience it. Both are ok as long as the dedication on lean is on to adapting the firm to market changes firmly. A firm becomes firm with lean by now or then. There are no special times like lean but lean is commonplace and not so common or only to common firms. But the fact remains that firms get to work on the lean as they need it and not when they want. Hence firms should keep an eye open towards lean because it can bring up its time anytime.

Today's lean is working towards the frontal development of the face of the firm in showing it as agile, energetic and

How Lean is Lean

guilt-free, but the real lean should not show anything on the front, rather the face of the firm becomes non-lean in real lean times; rest of the firm is lean still. A firm that is non-lean becomes stone-like and can be made lean by timely advocating of the operational excellence related strategies. The firms try to hit away the rivals but the markets don't let so. The insights from lean cannot be applied to ruin the competition otherwise healthy firms can become sick. Try to be lean as lean builds its own barriers and rules for the healthy business. The lean firm is not allowed to ruin itself or sway in adverse directions under any market conditions. The fact is that when firms go behind the demands of their ecosystems they get pulled in different directions from where they have to refine the core needs of the market at a given point in time.

How Lean is Lean

Lean firms don't let the rivals overcome their strategies for nothing. Either a lesson comes or a partner comes in such rivalry. The company culture evolves free of dilemmas or mind-sets of hollow types. The ground remained free for firms in the second half of 1900s when they would kill competitors with pricing or superstitious tactics to make them weak. The founders of Ford, GM, Sony and such firms were based on sound values in life so they could pass on to their firms with lean. Today if firms do the same, they won't succeed but fail as the founders are themselves not aligned to those values hence making them look like superstitions rather than beliefs. Even true firms with those values are called by other *unholy* firms as superstitious. It is not valid if a firm leaves a rival unharmed hoping for a better deal in the market. It is hoped that

How Lean is Lean

the firm hits the rival with a strong strategy that can't be reversed or stopped. Lean firms can do so without doing as any of the strategies soft or hard become strong to hit the rivals hard. Any market change or risk hits the firm on its brand image and hence that alone should not be lean. The corporate image need not be emulated as the rest of the company to be lean. The rivals also respond in such a way that aggressive move hits on the face of the company. Either place strong ambassadors or investors or let it be so strong that it can respond in similar ways to save the face. But still, firms must try not to get into face-saving situations as otherwise companies lose the lean focus and resources elsewhere. The present lean is tailored towards the frequent changes in the market without any textbook tweaking or tool wrenching. The default lean

How Lean is Lean

automatically updates to suit the times then and now as per the market situation and demand. It avails itself of the new changes and facilities of business world, it works on the rules of new game in corporate, and it mends to suit the workers and firms alike. So it is not a cause for worry if a lean does not seem to work in a time or situation. Lean works everywhere because a company is nothing without lean. The other concepts all came because companies failed to appreciate the importance of lean in the olden decades. It seems so at least because all other management tactics or concepts or tricks or tools are reactive and act on a sickness within a firm or are remedial. The firms did not pay enough attitudes to lean thus giving it for other ailing strategies. The one reason is also that lean is not easy.

How Lean is Lean

To be lean companies spend centuries in honing and unleashing useful energies. Lean believes in collaboration in times of difference or extreme ruination it advocates matching up to rivals rather than lose to market destruction. A lot of firms don't agree with it as earlier also firms wanted all progress and success for themselves without sharing anything with market. Today also firms want all profits and margins for them without ripping that market share for others. Lean rips the company to treat it of all ills. Hence the firms also give it a try to get lean as it does not always get a company great by altruistic business but by situation-based cooperation, coolness and competition.

Cool firms are firm and lean as they don't let the markets affect their internal decisioning or policies. Deferring to

How Lean is Lean

other companies or their policies does not make a firm lean or collaborative unless the conditions of markets demand. Stern companies are those that go on with lean but also risk the future agility as too much lean can get rid of agility. The firms hence need to go lean with alert competition answerable to key demands without losing the business focus to unwarranted conditions or responses. The firms must not stop from going lean as the risk of envy rises or the deviations all clutter around the company waiting for one missed chance to get it failed on non-lean grounds. A market had so many participants that they all wait for the leader or winner to sway in any direction and catch up wrong opportunities or prospects to divert focus onto inaccurate deals and dunkers. As the rivals expect the winning firm to stop growing its business by gathering junk business

How Lean is Lean

orders or involve in the muddle of ubiquitous business politics to avert resources in wrong channels, or take up progress along wrong decisions, lean firms avoid such traps or correct the inaccurate decisions to run the situations in their favour.

However, firms must still remember and write it on their gates that a single or a series of wrong decisions cannot force a business to collapse if the lean persists for recovery by hard-work, grit, determination on behalf of employees, founders, leaders and other stakeholders. It is again tough to administer this in a business as it is much more than eight letters. Hence a lean firm can do these stints better than others as every firm would face similar situations one or the other time in its existence. Hence the business

How Lean is Lean

philosophy says that resolving untimely challenges and facing them with focus can make the firm lean just as the reverse holds reasonable. It is easy to take up failure and sit back crying on the losses or red tapes but it is easier to resolve them if the firm is lean and goes for tapping the best of the lean. Lean does bring the success mould for the firm to fit in after it leans down though. The firms must go on with the lean and when they fall into the market sickness or cited slowdowns they must take adequate rest or relaxation to recover from the deadly hiccups posed by the internal or external environment.

It has to be known that the rest period is not meant for inactivity but to work on internal development of the firm. It can be good for the entire firm to take off on a vacation for a day by declaring as the

How Lean is Lean

family day for the firm. But hectic projects running through 365-24-7 do not get a firm to be lean or strong or winner. The firms have got the support systems built at every stage of their progress and they must use them to enable the efficiency at max and loss at minimum. Holding projects also does no good to the firm so the only option is to try lean to balance the growth vs. rest vs. risky times. The firms must hence tackle the times to ensure lean in lot of ways at all times to shield the firm from losses of all forms.

How Lean is Lean

14- Lean impact on Sales

Firms anyway rest all arguments on sales at the end of quarter or year. Financial tools and statements are present to evaluate the progress of firm over time but not for discrete tracking or pin-pointing of business lacunae. Financial part assumes the firm is growing and progressive or lean enough to face the paper. But fat firms often put them in the wrong shoes to get the sales as the single parameter to judge lean. The impact of lean is on every business element including sales. Lean does not however promise a rise in sales as that is contingent upon various other factors, not just the lean. The concern from day 1 of company is sales in one form or the other as revenue, margins, clients, costs, volumes etc. Firms don't get instant revenues but have to complete the entire product or process or service

How Lean is Lean

cycles to get them ready for sale. When a product sells, it is the company that sells. Firms get clear till here. They miss out or ignore that customers are buying the company even with a single product purchase in their lifetimes. The stakes are high so firms that value customers know that once they are bought, they are in the hands of customers forever. A product is in premises for less than 20% of the time and with customers for more than 80% of its existence. How can one sell the next product to the same or referred client if the previous purchase did not buy in her loyalty or the next one? At some purchase the customer has to get aligned to the company's products and recommend to others or buy it on every need. The lean helps companies manage the hidden aspect of sales without beating around the money or profit. Even if profits don't come for a decade its ok if the

How Lean is Lean

customers let the business run in the ecosystem. Even if the firm mines 50% margins in the first week, it is of no use if the buyers do not want it to continue on the stands. That is when acquisitions or takeovers or mergers happen. Or the companies exit the sector in a year or two. Sellers can hire experts for convincing buyers but they finally sell the company and not just products.

The entire team, project, technology and operation along with the mission of the firm gets passed to the customer. A product is manufactured in anyway but those firms that take care in product handling or testing win the mileage with buyers for longer than those who merely view them as machine thrown lots. This mission-set is editing the minds of buyers when they buy a product as it works without letting any side be aware

How Lean is Lean

of the facts. The results show on the decision or perception or the next buys. Lean gives the sense of production to the firms and buyers who admire the effort gone in it to go ahead for the delight. It is the human beings who use the products though they may be churned by machines. So companies have to put their act together on the policy or process front to involve as much human effort as possible, at least 10% if it is perfect and efficient. This means that the inspection or packaging or sampling needs to be done internally by giving the products to a limited segment of employees or external dummy shoppers for real use at homes. Even before, the product must pass on the real hands via raw material or phase-wise item scrutiny or playing with the things by a top manager who is well-versed with the entire cycles and business. It is done to some extent but

How Lean is Lean

stopped after it gains brand equity. Lean says that it must be consistent and wholesome to get the product rolling in the lives of people it has to be rolled in the lives of sellers. Today every product is promoted by a celebrity so how much probability can each stand to win against others without getting the flavour of employee dedication rather than sales addiction seen in it? We can smell the intent behind every product but no market has stopped any firm from hailing the intent to human though the end-result may be and is money. Only very few, I repeat, countable on fingers, companies do it for their sales. They do not want to compromise the brand or take risk by admitting human values to their business but that happens for sure as any company will have to face the challenges whether on ethics or otherwise. So it is better to be upfront with the customer as that imbibes the

How Lean is Lean

culture within the company instead of one off product building activity.

The companies edit the tag line and it is the face of the product but the fact remains that in the subconscious of buyers the firm is the face of the product. The entire effort becomes the traveller with the product when it goes to buyer. The mission, policies and processes all have to include the salt of human essence into the product right from the start. Even totally machine-made products will have to face the feedback of customers and managers have to justify their positions. Firms create challenges for themselves when they take business and work for it. They get into issues when they don't pay enough heed to customers or don't justify their products. Lean helps know and manage the customer depth for the

How Lean is Lean

products. Each product has different colours indicating different levels of involvement of different types of customers. There are end-users, mid-processors, dependent customers who need it as a raw material for some other form, facilitators who give the product or distribute it with rights and due licenses to the others by holding the products in their arena. Banks do that when they have all the products but give the authority to their customers for investing and getting returns from them. Like that there revel all industries that work on the sales and must adopt lean to get buyer interest. The margins settle on their own if the product gets an appeal with the customers or their friends. A member may not like it but her family might be using the product because it fits with their images nipping their fears or flaws in life. When a product connects to this level of usage then it gets sold for good.

How Lean is Lean

A good automatic electronic razor gives confidence to the manager that he can groom himself in minutes even if outside or without power or in a busy meeting or urgent one with clients. He retains it in his pocket or travel kit for easy access and hence the product is adding value to his work as he can use it anywhere in free time without allocating separately for it. When the company made it, it may have thought of the exactly same benefits that the customer can feel now, if the company had merely thought about the technology and price or value alone then it would have passed the same to the customers and they can get there without even using it. The connect is not between company and customers but product and buyers. The companies feel that the products must excite and challenge users to provide ideas, criticism or praise for the products routed on a given service. The lean

How Lean is Lean

precisely points out when a buyer buys only the product or the entire experience and such a buyer becomes a sale himself as he sells his choice to others. It is not easy to reach here and companies have fought for centuries without getting to any major scale on the relation with customers. One or two may claim the 80% revenues or consistent business for decades with the single client but that is not really admirable. That indicates risk with high risk-low return as a single client cannot pay higher but only lower prices with each year of loyalty on the lines of being loyal discount entity for the firm. If the client is defunct once, then the firm is gone for good. It is preferable that a firm have multiple customers creating new ones instead of one repeating the business. Some customers may exit the bag by passing on the product to others when they upgrade or shift or stop using the

How Lean is Lean

feature when the need stops arising. There are customers that pass on the product lineage to others in the family or friends. It manages and retains the use of the product without disturbing the buyers' reliabilities. This can happen if the company also and not only the product is sold to the buyer. Nobody can if given a chance also ignore the company culture if it emerges strong in the product as it enhances the speed or thinking or lifestyle of users. We don't mind if the price is low or high if it is adding more value than we need. The dollar stores sometimes sell better products than high end stores and hence buyers pick on those products that meet their needs well. A family buys the same soap for generations because they see the value and emotion behind the product suiting their needs and familiarity. Even the friends and relatives start on the same product because if

How Lean is Lean

one has stuck to it for decades then it must have some value to it. Thus the lineage builds around a product and the corporate culture behind it. The impact of product must be assessed as that of the company on the buyers or customers or users and not just as a sales management.

The lean manages the intricate cycle of sales to make it available to the extended circles of the customers rather than a single one. As it becomes non-lean, customers start moving away from that firm's deliverables on grounds of getting affected in pricing or utility or business sense as the grounds or pretexts create several contexts for ignoring a product but none in favour. Again lending lean sales does not guarantee sales but precludes reasons for not selling. The sales are the key areas of observation and trending but market does a lot more than that. They

How Lean is Lean

want the lean to create magic on sales by getting the employees and customers run after the products. Employees run behind the products to make them better and innovative by each transition. Customers run behind the products to get them into their life to get compatible with the companies as then their voice would be heard more by the firms investing millions in research and big data. They do so because lean showers a negative impact on sales. This happens because there is always a gap between market and internal environment leading to scope for improvement for the firm. Thus lean is on a path of constant up gradation or innovation or change for firms, employees and customers. Lean eliminates all negative reasons stopping the sales leaving the market open to the advancement and grilling of the quality for further innovation. Under most

How Lean is Lean

certain conspiring conditions the slack goes away and the sales happen but there is still an open crevice of buyers not giving loyalties to the product or firm for some personal or unknown reasons. Such conditions don't drive the firms into deprivation or market failure as they have the lean support to persist in the sale that is bound to occur without further embankment on valid or invalid reasons. As more than anything, the buyers start valuing the sales as worthy of emulating the company ideals in their life. That comes without saying and products move in to the behavioural or attitudinal prevention of lifestyle deterioration. A product adds social status and internal satisfaction to the user who is able to reach to higher career and personal goals with the help of the lean products mined by the lean firms. Lean thus prepares the entire fraternity to become lean to get the best results mined in surprise and need based utility. Today we see students and professionals reacting equally randomly to the new products and offers on markets but they can be aligned or controlled with the help of lean. Companies need to use lean to avoid the customers from taking random or wrong decisions on superficial levels in favour of a competitor and against the real good products. Command comes with lean as the firms tell others that their work and products mean and lead to the same values that customers also admire in their life. The products meet their need but the use meets their life. The lean impact on sales can be said to own the product as a multi-lifestyle enchantment put across the customer to give and take value in the form of features and comments as applicable. It makes the sales also lean in that they are not fretting for numbers but trust and

How Lean is Lean

dependency of customers on the company. Sales can run out and take the company into closure. Trust can renovate the company from weak sales into defiant adherence to customer and that trust is filled by the non-biased lean.

15 - Everyone's a Customer

The reasons for not excelling in business are lack of knowledge, understanding and experience with customers. Let us define who a customer ultimately is for a company. In lean everyone is a customer. In onerous non-lean nobody is a customer rather they drift from the business. For any company it if works with everyone as a customer then it excels in all areas of business. A customer is not only the one who pays for it but also who uses it or tries it or comments on it. The first customer of a company is its employee. The next is the investor or shareholder followed by the sponsors or top leaders or founders who always find customers for customers. The others are the distributors who are first external customers of the companies. If they are convinced about the company then they

How Lean is Lean

can do so with other users. For other reasons, intermediaries are not good but if the margin can be managed then these can create wonders by their access into the nooks of customer segments and face-to-face acquaintance with customers including fluency and local ownership. Lending lean does mend the links on supply chain to allow a healthy participation of all stakeholders as where the dealers can reach, firms cannot and will not. There are two ends of Salesforce and Autoforce where the firms deal with internal dealers or external local dealers. Cars can never sell if the firms take upon the task however great a car may be or cheap it may be. The dealers have and will be on their value chains as they add the buyers like nobody else can. The internet or corporate floors opening up the sales can also not replace the dealers who generate a

How Lean is Lean

rapport to create a life-long experience for the customer whether she buys or not. The lean must ensure that such links are able to bring back some data in terms of what they prefer or not, like or not, want or not etc. The not's are important because firms often make and sell extra that are not given the price as they don't add value at all. Weeding out the differences among customers themselves is a huge next lean. The different layers of consumers are bent on varying purchase parameters like price, quality, life, features etc. Some companies restrict to a layer while other firms work with different products for each tier of customers. These include physical as well as online outputs. And buyers value them without cribbing about a better product for a higher price or a different quality at a lower price. Every key influencer or effector on company or its produce is a customer.

How Lean is Lean

Each single customer is a customer of new customers as she builds up a network of new participants in the business sales or cycles. One customer in Africa has influenced her friends so lot that one joined the firm, another started a franchise, a family member became seller within the relatives and they all are branding the product in their customers areas without even the company knowing it as firms do not recognize such isolated groups but here goes the fact that such loyalties create new segments of customers without fail when they put up the views on blogs or posts or internet or mobile chats. Depending on the usage and impact a customer is more risky or less. Importance is equal as she can harm the sales if not loyal. The risk comes with the customer and is high if she is a more loyal one because her switch to a different firm can eliminate her friends

How Lean is Lean

from the loyalty rungs too. Here it is again true that a one-time customer is less in risk but she must be converted into regular one to get the permanent customer base even if risky. Risks must be managed but not avoided in order for the business to be growing and performing in excellence. The consultants are also in the category of customers because they buy into the corporate ideologies to come up with their recommendation on business growth and lean. If they don't accept the corporate values then they don't come up clean on their lean strategies. And it is known fact that external consultants charge a fee for nothing or something just for their time and ideas whether they are used or not. Lean thus manages the customers in different forms and corners of the business ecosystem by getting them aligned not on the products but on the principles

How Lean is Lean

governing the company. This may be vocal or indirect or subtle but it persists for all business areas through all times.

The lean practice brags about customers more than the products but that does not mean endless testimonials or references or praise songs for the products. It means that the customers are levied with the job of criticising their companies with gut and freedom to cultivate trust and confidence in the long-term.

16 - Customers compete

The best scenario of lean is when segments of customers compete along the lines of the business that they are looking at to assist with sales, fabrication and pre-production. Lean can make that happen as companies and lean work for the clients on the markets. As they excel in one process, the price of lean becomes dear and the stakes are high with a higher turnover if lean is taken to other business processes and areas too when the old customers also try to imbibe some of the favourable traits of their firms into their products and then into lives. The needs are modified and influenced by the good company traits or characteristics that enable the gift of lean to be presented to the next level of their lifestyle. Customers learn about the lean in its differentiated forms like the corporate

How Lean is Lean

values, product clan, process tan and growth plan. They also adopt the same in their lives and compare with other customers using other companies. The canal of loyalty does not stop here but courses to create new channels of expansion and growth of user bases for the companies in lean. If the lean is not real, or coincidental or not a constant process, then the torrent of returns or deluge on rival shifts or famine of criticism, may occur to sink the boat of the business along with the stakeholders. Lean makes the customers compete for excellence in their lives shooing the worst and wooing the best of life. They get to the stage where they become voices of firms to form support sectors of like-product segments. Business has no mind but the product that is common with the customers. Hence the product becomes the mind of users nestling the sellers.

How Lean is Lean

The lean to be specific becomes the mind of the business as it guides that sustainability and growth for the firms involved in it. Give a piece of lean and everybody will take it. It gives the required stability and decision control to the business in the ever volatile times and capricious markets. The future face of lean is going to be competition between the customers when the firm's task gets less than 10% importance. Once the products are done and rolled in the markets the task of firms passes to the beholders or users of products. If lean they would give it a long standing otherwise the products lose the market in a short span of time as also many a time, the buyers are seen comparing and competing on their reviews but it is going to go one step ahead with usages. The usage would be on bets in the future lean where companies and their customers would create campaigns of

How Lean is Lean

free or fee to leave product in the arena of trial or test for prolonged chunks of time and varieties. This is to say that the prototyping itself would be lending the lean to the markets and hence branding would start rather than form at the end as of now. Today customers create brands after recognition of the product value. Tomorrow, companies will see branding happening by customers in the roll-out of plans as they help the firms in fashioning the ideas into useable samples and then freezing into products after getting the complete buy-in; the cycles is running from backwards to front but it works as then the companies would have to invest even in the addition of value of samples to final products and customers would be involved at all the phases of the cycle. New customers strive to get into the usage segments of the companies already doing well in the old sectors.

How Lean is Lean

Some switches happen as old firms lose their users to the better lean firms. Lean firms leave the ground free for user to enter and exit thus constructing it simple to follow or leave the ground. This makes more loyal customers than those trying to hold or bind the customers. Retention is possible if the customer desire is favourable. That happens when firms are lean to let free of their buyers to decide between real and erred products.

The lean does not enforce any rules of rewards but of excellence so it is not a goal game but process game. It is the resort because we have exhausted all goals and measures. Now we are left with the process and business routes to success for making better of the firms and customers. If the companies do not see the criticism or fiasco they wont learn to experiment and risk the designs due to which the best ones won't evolve

How Lean is Lean

by time if firms stick to a notion to get normal gains. So lean has to be adopted to know the best from the worst in markets, customers, products and competitors. Customers are not all well-informed, decisive or bipartisan. They are as much driven by the woes of life as the ads of rivals. Hence a clear path has to be paved by the firms in front of the customers to get them view the quality without any haze. Only true and excellent firms can risk that otherwise the loopholes would kill their company if pointed by the buyers. Lean gives the excellence and ethic to the firm to let it stand without any fear of loss, defect or waste. It gives the firm also the ability to view clearly its status in the market and clarify any misconceptions or wrong perceptions of users to get right the mistakes or faults or risks posed by internal or external environments in the business ecosystem or economic

How Lean is Lean

frontiers supporting or opposing the industrial trends or directions. The firms lose out on even the macro signals because they are in market haze and on a confused evolution left on luck and bonus. Lean clarifies a lot of miasma twisted by the participants and stakeholders or competitors of the business. It is needed for getting enthusiastic users instead of forced buyers for long-run benefits and growth.

17 - Who is a Customer?

Let's define the customer. **A customer is anybody who creates cusp with tomorrow for your business ergonomics**. She guides your business by relating with others. A customer who leaves your product is also important to

How Lean is Lean

you as she has the secret for rejection. Why would she reveal it if you ignore her saying, you are not my customer but someone other's? It does not mean that you have to call customers as so because you need data from them. They are indeed creating the business needs for tomorrow and generating a tight ergonomics for your business today. They can only link the journey with tomorrow. They can advance your company from today to tomorrow. Their feedback can affect your company in many directions as they write the comparisons without using your product. **Anybody who can affect your business is your customer.** Payment or no payment, sale or no sale… she is still your customer if she can do a wee bit with your company. A customer is a clue used to sustain tools of my entity as a right. The customers give you the right to remain in the maker business. They

How Lean is Lean

are the clues for business progress. They are never the whole because they don't participate in a lot of activities like business growth, decisioning, primary market etc. Not one of these can proceed without their indirect nod.

Lean asks you who is your customer at each stage of business evolution and gets the details right on how to manage the rows of customers at each phase. It is not always the investors who want direct monetary return, they do want more money in return for their money but customers also want return for their purchase. If the return is in the product itself then they don't look for more but or else they want rewards and loyalty gifts. Imagine a company that is perfect and able to time and price the perfect products to delight the customers. They won't ask for anything more then as they

How Lean is Lean

are satisfied and the persistence for more comes only when the given product does not satisfy them to any full. Then the buyers will create the gap between price and value as they get the products used in their life. The gap is formed as the firms sell the goods and lean can help vouch for a gapless product so that the real loyalty comes from customers rather than a chain pull of rewards, extras, perks and all that go with imperfect products or incomplete services.

The customer is one who gets a complete product rather than a single product and then a reward now and more later. Custom products also help lean fit needs to sales but customers form the custom of the company, and the custom of the company is to sell. Firms must try to grow the customers as being able to become the custom of the purchase. Customers are followers of

How Lean is Lean

the custom of buying or using. The sellers follow the custom of building useable products. The assembly of buyers and sellers is lean if buyers get lean inputs. The outputs of companies are the inputs for the customers. The lean inputs encourage them to adopt lean in their lifestyle thus mandating the use of lean products in the future also. This emanates allegiance so that the customers don't use any tethering product that does not propagate lean but is chosen out of other concerns like pricing, feature, guarantees etc. A lean product brings in all these allied factors, which have to be worked on by non-lean firms. Working on each leaves the scope undefined and risk open for firms to falter on the finished good. Working on the lean approach, tests all other parameters, in one lot, by tying the parameters to the finished good, as if to get it through. A lot of firms prefer the

How Lean is Lean

lean as one for all rather than multiple approaches for each attribute. Some say that we have lot of other things to do in our companies and cant spend the life in lean. Lean ensures all other things too as it opens up the entire business path to success and growth on amplified levels to let firms appreciate the importance of every approach and parameter. Lean is like the religion of business which if practised can create tolerance for all other business frameworks if suitable or chuck out the unworthy ones that only waste resource without creating that value for the use. It has to be accepted that the value for money would be taken by the lean to give value to use rather than price or bucks. The customer buys a product because no other product is able to meet her need. Hence the use gains proportion of relative importance and that has to be for the value of the user. If

How Lean is Lean

not, she may move to another product or competition. That is why a company so often promotes a range of products meeting a single need to retain the customer by allowing use in various forms instead of one. A customer is the controller of business in true sense as she holds the usage right that nobody can enforce. A firm can make her buy the product but not use it. Lean ensures that the usage seems so important to the life that customer wants the product again and again for a product not used is of no use even if bought by force or flair. Lean moves to the ultimate step of usage that associates a customer with the product and the company tightly. Lean tells you to sell the usage as if you can get the buyer use it then he would buy it anyway. Companies do that but as a choice as they don't trust or expect you to use if a product is bought as the employees are rewarded only for

How Lean is Lean

making the sale and the buck stops ever. The targets are not on returns or exchanges or the use but tied to the plain vanilla sales or only the conversions. That is why lean does not rely on such hollow measures of success. It cannot enforce the employee beyond a strain level so it works on customers to get real product or complete service to attain the usage proficiency or aptitude. The usage aptitude is cultivated by lean after the products are tapped into everlasting quality ones. Once the employees are giving full potential to the products they can then be projected before users for their usage. Or the products can pull them into business process for the feedback on the prototypes or to-be quality so that the final goods are tuned and toned to usage patterns. Lean gives the immense value to the use as

How Lean is Lean

measure of loyalty of buyers or company success.

Refer lean to customers and they will refer the firm to the other buyers. Refer lean to employees and they will defer the efficiency to quality. Quality is a common attribute today but the utility with efficiency behind the quality can render uniqueness to the product.

How Lean is Lean

0 - Lean Employees

The lean comes back to employees as the entire process and product and project is of no service to buyer if the bucks pass without the passing of business bucks. Buck me no more buck. The onus of lean is on employees and the outcome is on buyers when they buy into company products to add on their friends or family with the real touch of the corporate values held behind the lean. Thus the company etches out a multi-layer recognition based on products, going deep into the lean and deeper into the policies or values behind. Hence it gives a binding of market space and brand equity when lean harmonizes between the product and the values. As the employees craft fervour for lean the products pass the same gust to high end or low end customers irrespective of the price they

How Lean is Lean

pay. The lean thus forms a pledge in their lifestyles that are generated out of the products assembled by lean firms. The utility is for customers and company just as the efficiency should also be for users and not just within the company premises. The high utility product may have been gotten on the most efficient processes but when it goes to the customer it hardly serves as it delays the charging or operation per se and it is not adding efficiency to the user. The lean value is the immense strong one that lasts for lifetime to enable the customers get the full faith in the company along with the products as if the core need is satisfied then others are weeded out or drizzled on the extras earning brand value. If the lean is not in the employees then they address the needs in a random fashion and may even at times skip the core need that the customers may be not really aware

How Lean is Lean

of. The lean culture can initiate customers and others to follow the products of the company if the employees don't find anything else working. When all else fails, lean hails leans. The products that we use in our daily life also enter the life passing the product culture into our values and life strategies. If the employees can be nurtured with this principle then they can bring out better innovation to get away with non-lean elements of the business. A non-lean employee uses such practice to churn out such product that turns customer into grumpy and diffident user. The attributes may not be directly blamed but she finds comfort in another product and uses it or feels it as most of us buy on the feel rather than detailed microscopic inspection or product bioscopy by magnifying glass or dissection of features. That is why ads are meant to create that aura with

How Lean is Lean

ambassadors and ambience around the product. With time, we have become cleverer and stopped buying in the glitters of stars with a product. Rather the buyer lot has risen up to the levels to get closer to the companies to understand what they are selling and why. This is all on the product aura that we are trying to feel as customers. I don't think this product will sell a lot or do a lot is the usual feedback on ads. Earlier I think the good ad seems to bring out the goodness in the product was the usual view but products started betraying their ad auras. So all that is left to feel, is on the real gene that is passed to the consumer along with product. Does it enhance or deplete the life patterns of consumer including the social appeal and internal well-being. As finally it is the users that have to binge on the economic growth so that the credit can go to their circadian products

How Lean is Lean

or services enhancing their life amidst the competition and tension built into their life. The activities of company hence correlate to those of the consumers and innovation points out the same as a gap between the need and product. The desire of customers may not be their need, and the salient need may not be the wish of the employees. Hence the balance is generated by lean that works on the wish, need, desire and deliverable of employees. Thus lean employees are the stepping stones to the lean economies. Lean firms come from lean employees and hence all growth comes from the trained or skilled lean workers who incorporate the lean into operations, processes, tasks, routines, manuals, maintenance, testing, overhaul, techniques, strategies and gimmicks that go behind the products or deliverables, with amenities, hand-outs or solutions. Fringe benefits are not at

How Lean is Lean

all hunted by true customers who get true products but markets have ardently waited for such products only to come and go once in a decade or so. Tired consumers accept what they get at a time and few innovative companies market to the delight but if lean is adopted then all firms can try to gain some of the consistent and sustainable business in today's advanced world of technology and hectic competition.

The employees can be cross-utilized between sectors if they are lean rather than a technology expert. One machine does not serve all sectors but one lean employee can contribute to all sectors by identifying the weak areas, filling the gaps in lean, taking the business to the better growth areas, convincing customers to be lot more loyal and inclined towards the companies and

How Lean is Lean

sectors rather than prices or offers. If offers are the only things that we run after then all companies would see offers running out but that does not always happen. Some companies see the offers expiring without subscription. The unsold stocks are wasted or dumped in exports. If the stock is not perishable then they are repackaged or rediscounted for further sale as the lean is missing here. True lean does not let the stocks to accumulate beyond the need as we have all the tools and softwares to churn out needed products and calculate the need based on demand forecasting technologies. It is human to err and technological to err as the logic of machine also cannot predict the psyche of the buyer. Hence the lean averts focus from the abstract sales to the real involvement in the company. The sales numbers are once too often deceptive and the company is not. The

How Lean is Lean

customer if likes the company can leave all deception at bay to forego the discounts or offers in lieu of the natural product brought out of lean.

How Lean is Lean

Conclusion: The Closing Insignia

The nations are playing on industries and dependent on the industrial growth than agricultural or services sectors irrespective of the contribution and shape of the economy.

The lean economies are the ones to sustain like the lean companies as all growth tends to be with the fast and flexible. Lean is necessary to prove the worth of slow and steady as sustainability is only over a long period and not instant. Internet and technologies have made us instantaneous and the economies instant. The companies all seek remedies instantly and the nations grow along with the same development track. The industries cannot force economy to sway the track but they can provide a better benchmark and mode of growth. Firms are present in all sectors whether

How Lean is Lean

primary, secondary or tertiary. The agri-firms, consumer firms, and professional firms are prone to inefficiencies neither traceable nor remediable. Hence lean would help in controlling to the extent of wastage and in enhancing to the world of productivity. Coping with defects and wastes with most output is the worst problem of the century. Companies are netting out their losses on the pretext of abnormal contingencies or on the grounds of non-controllable risks of market. But the fact is that the dwindling growth traces the poor performance to lean failure whether in known form on invisible. The rising growths of economies indicate that the success of lean somewhere in the known or totally free circles of the economy. The sectors can be improved because whether home or office, the issues are common. The concept is universal whether applied as one framework or as an

How Lean is Lean

independent process. It is prevalent at various levels in our growth on all fronts both on personal and business areas. In a way, the wealth accumulated in all nations is the sum total of all lean efforts and the original productivity. The growth is less if the lean part is small as the original growth is more or less standardised for groups of nations or regions. The growth is more when the lean contribution is full. But that is the gap. Lean is never full and there is always some or the other gap leading to scope for improvement in the future business. The directions for growth are men, material and machines. Money is anyway not ignored by any business whether for inflows or outflows. This is where the extra surplus is generated to make the nations advanced or developing or recessive. The surplus growth makes the nations make wealth in their economies. Our job is to get

How Lean is Lean

efficiency by lean and search it in all other places and forms where it is applied. Then only the world will become a better place for business with growth. Whether quality, process, value-chain, products or contributors, the lean has to be made a favourite of all and reaped of its gains.

The game of the firm-industry-nation has to be understood through lean as that gives the lens of unbiased consumer and producer in the economy. The linear growth becomes dense if the lean is effective in all domains of the economic development and it starts with industry because out and out our lifestyles are getting dunked in products and durables. They are of different types and varieties on brands and goodwill. The surplus or deficits influence the economic activity locally and globally.

How Lean is Lean

The global growth comes from domestic excellence and vice versa. Lean helps build the affluence on both ends when it gets the domestic business efficient and gears global users fast. Lean should be viewed as a friend of economy rather than a substitute of failure or stimulator of growth. It does both but the initial perception influences how it is administered in business and how the results flow out of it later. Economy indeed depends on efficiency for productivity to be maximum level and yield to be of excellent quality. Energy comes from lean as the resources get into the pockets of business only as much as they are needed and utilized. The rest goes into the building of future business grounds by the companies and economies. It is true that a surplus or deficit in a firm or industry can influence the levels at economic growth.
Everybody knows that the reverse holds

How Lean is Lean

true more than any other macro factor. The lean grows the economy into a compact and mobile engine for the global growth. We have to reach that stage, whoever the nation may be. The drivers are all open in the technological era as the nations are racing towards prosperity. The wealth is in terms of monetary, industrial, agricultural or services growth. With mobile technologies, the onus shifts on the economies to dangle with the non-lean or ineffective strategies by using lean. Lean economies become mobile economies to be big enough and still agile to move along the global shift and sift. It passes on the strength or pre-forecasting capabilities to firms, sectors and regions thus making the economy strong and motivated towards rewards, welfare, merit and recognition of its citizens. It is not right to say that some resources are futile or some men are

How Lean is Lean

useless. It is true in financial parlance only that NPAs exist for that time or segment. In an economy, every resource is an asset and just needs to be recognized of how to utilize it for the maximum value addition to the nation and world. Let not the nations compute but compete on lean. That would bring in a world of balance between globalization, localization, efficiency, customization, environments or green, and create the real wealth for future progress as today is short but future is long. An economy free of inefficiencies is lean liberated enough to take up new challenges to create new models of evolution or solution for other economies as we all know how one economy can shake or wake others in no time on no related parameters or dependencies.

How Lean is Lean

Take a little care of lean and lean will take full care of you and your entire economy.

www.ingramcontent.com/pod-product-compliance
Lightning Source LLC
Chambersburg PA
CBHW070222190526
45169CB00001B/44